REA

FRIE
3 1833 0
OF A
D0678093

the insider's guide for
NEW TEACHERS

SARA BUBB

RoutledgeFalmer
Taylor & Francis Group

LONDON AND NEW YORK

JAN 1 3 2005

First published in Great Britain and the United States in 2003 by Kogan Page Limited

Apart from any fair dealing for the purposes of research or private study, or criticism or review, as permitted under the Copyright, Designs and Patents Act 1988, this publication may only be reproduced, stored or transmitted, in any form or by any means, with the prior permission in writing of the publishers, or in the case of reprographic reproduction in accordance with the terms and licences issued by the CLA. Enquiries concerning reproduction outside these terms should be sent to the publishers at the undermentioned addresses:

Reprinted 2004
by RoutledgeFalmer
11 New Fetter Lane, London, EC4P 4EE

Simultaneously published in the USA and Canada
by RoutledgeFalmer
29 West 35th Street, New York, NY 10001

RoutledgeFalmer is an imprint of the Taylor & Francis Group

© Sara Bubb, 2003

The right of Sara Bubb to be identified as the author of this work has been asserted by her in accordance with the Copyright, Designs and Patents Act 1988.

ISBN 0 7494 4101 1

The views expressed in this book are those of the author and are not necessarily the same as those of *The Times Educational Supplement*.

British Library Cataloguing-in-Publication Data
A CIP record for this book is available from the British Library.

Library of Congress Cataloging-in-Publication Data
Bubb, Sara
   The insider's guide for new teachers : succeed in training and
induction / Sara Bubb.
      p. cm.
Includes bibliographical references and index.
   ISBN 0-7494-4101-1
   1. First year teachers--Handbooks, manuals, etc. 2. Teacher
orientation--Handbooks, manuals, etc. 3. Teaching--Handbooks, manuals,
etc. I. Title.
   LB2844.1.N4B82 2003
   371.1--dc21
                              2003010393

Printed and bound in Great Britain by MPG Books Ltd, Bodmin, Cornwall

Contents

Preface

The *Times Educational Supplement* Web site's New Teacher Forum is one busy little corner of the virtual staffroom that gets 5,000 hits a week, and the postings vary between 100 and 264 a week. There are lots of different queries that I and others try our best to answer. Having been the *TES* new teacher agony aunt for two years, I've seen that lots of new teachers' concerns are on similar themes. So this book tries to help with those tricky bits of a new teacher's life, to offer the sort of help, clear information and practical tips that you are crying out for.

Being a new teacher is like learning to do anything new. It's a journey, the first stages of which are the hardest and that's what I hope to help you with. This book isn't trying to replace the support, monitoring and assessment that will be essential features of your training and induction but I hope that it oils their wheels, and lets you know where the potholes and traffic jams are, so that you don't just survive but succeed.

This book is unusual in being aimed at new teachers – both trainees and NQTs. Both groups have similarly tough journeys. I've written the book in two parts: the first primarily about training to be a teacher and the second on surviving your first year, although Chapter 4 'Looking after yourself' is important for people at both – if not all – stages of their career. Part 1 starts with advice and information on choosing a course and goes on to explain what you have to do to get qualified teacher status; in particular, the dreaded skills tests. Then I write about those elements of being on a training course that have been the topic of most queries: criminal record and health declarations, study skills, writing essays, planning lessons, marking, managing behaviour, learning from other teachers, and making the most of being observed. Obviously, many of these will be relevant to NQTs as well.

Part 2 covers the start of the first year as a teacher. It begins by examining all the factors to consider when looking for a job: what sort of school to choose, financial incentives, and where to look. Chapter 6 looks into what you have to do to get a job – the application and interview process and the all-important detective work. In Chapter 7, salary structure is explained and tips are offered for setting up your classroom and dealing with parents. The last two chapters are on induction. The first outlines the rules – focussing on England, but referring to Wales and Scotland where differences are important – so that you know how you are meant to be treated. The last chapter gives you detailed advice on how to make the most of induction support, monitoring and assessment. I am a firm believer that induction can really help you speed up that journey to being the greatest teacher that ever was.

I know that you're busy people, with lots of reading to do, so I've tried to write in an accessible and to the point style. I've used real extracts from postings (mostly anonymous, of course) to the New Teacher Forum in the 'Inbox' boxes to give you a real feeling for the issues you may come up against, as well as some useful tips. Click on the New Teacher Forum (http://www.tes.co.uk/staffroom/index.asp) and see what friendly and helpful people visit it. I've been amazed at people's kindness: sharing experiences and even, in one memorable case, working out exactly what a new teacher's take-home pay would be after stoppages.

I hope you enjoy reading this book, and find it useful. Learn from the concerns and situations that others have found themselves in so that your first years in teaching are successful – not just survived.

Acknowledgements

This book has been written as a practical guide for trainee and newly qualified teachers. As such, I would like to thank all the people who make contributions on the New Teacher Forum at the *Times Educational Supplement* Web site and everyone who comes to my courses at the University of London Institute of Education and at the Lewisham, Lambeth, Greenwich, Medway and Jersey Professional Development Centres. My past and present PGCE students and overseas trained teachers at the Institute must also be acknowledged, because they have given me such insights into how people learn to be teachers. I hope this book will help them get a good start in teaching.

Thanks to all who have helped and encouraged me, especially Peter Earley from the Institute of Education, John Carr from the Teacher Training Agency, Stephen Jones from Kogan Page and Susan Young from the *TES*.

Most of all, I must thank Paul, Julian, Miranda and Oliver for their encouragement and tolerance of me while I wrote this book.

List of abbreviations

AB	Appropriate Body
AHT	Assistant Headteacher
AST	Advanced Skills Teacher
ATL	Association of Teachers and Lecturers
BEd	Bachelor of Education
BT	Beginning Teacher
CEDP	Career Entry and Development Profile
CEO	Chief Education Officer of an LEA
CPD	Continuing Professional Development
CPS	Common Pay Spine
CTC	City Technology College
DfES	Department for Education and Skills
DHT	Deputy Headteacher
DRB	Designated Recommending Body
EAL	English as an Additional Language
EAZ	Education Action Zone
EBD	Emotional and Behavioural Difficulties
EiC	Excellence in Cities
EMA	Ethnic and Minority Achievement
EWO	Education Welfare Officer
G&T	Gifted and Talented
GTC	General Teaching Council (for England)
GTP	Graduate Teacher Programme
GTTR	Graduate Teacher Training Registry
HEI	Higher Education Institution
HMI	Her Majesty's Inspectorate
HoD	Head of Department
HoF	Head of Faculty
HT	Headteacher
ICT	Information & Communications Technology

IEP	Individual Education Plan for pupils with SEN
INSET	In-Service Education and Training
ISCTIP	Independent Schools Council Teacher Induction Panel
ITE	Initial Teacher Education
ITT	Initial Teacher Training
LEA	Local Education Authority
LGA	Local Government Association
LPSH	Leadership Programme for Serving Headteachers
LT	Leadership Team
MFL	Modern Foreign Languages
MPS	Main Pay Scale
NAS	National Association of Schoolteachers
NLS	National Literacy Strategy
NNS	National Numeracy Strategy
NPQH	National Professional Qualification for Headship
NQT	Newly Qualified Teacher
NUT	National Union of Teachers
OFSTED	Office for Standards in Education
PGCE	Postgraduate Certificate in Education
QCA	Qualifications and Curriculum Authority
QTS	Qualified Teacher Status
RB	Recommending Body
RTL	Repayment of Teacher Loans
RTP	Registered Teacher Programme
SCITT	School-Centred Initial Teacher Training
SEN	Special Educational Needs
SENCO	Special Educational Needs Coordinator
SMT	Senior Management Team
STRB	School Teachers' Review Body
TES	*Times Educational Supplement*
TP	Teaching Practice
TPS	Teachers' Pay Scale
TTA	Teacher Training Agency
UCAS	Universities and Colleges Admissions Service

part one

Training

one

Getting on a training course

- Entry requirements
- Routes to being a qualified teacher
- If you trained to be a teacher overseas
- Financial incentives
- The application form
- Interviews

So, you've decided to be a teacher. Great! Despite all the recruitment problems and the advertising to tempt you into the profession, choosing and getting on the right training course for you is not easy, despite teacher shortages. Every year committed people are turned down. This chapter will give you information about entry requirements, all the numerous routes you can go down and their financial incentives. It has tips on completing application forms and being successful at interview.

Entry requirements

The entry requirements to get onto any teaching course are fixed, and you need to make sure you meet them before even thinking about applying. The Teacher Training Agency (TTA) Teaching Information Line should be your first port of call (0845 6000991 or 6000992 for Welsh speakers). For instance, you'll need to get studying if you don't have GCSE maths or English at C grade or above. You can apply for a QTS (Qualified Teacher Status) course before the results are known so long as the exam date is fixed, but obviously, people with the qualifications already will have an advantage. (Entry requirements are the same in Northern Ireland as those in England and Wales.)

Entry requirements

All QTS training providers must:

- satisfy themselves that all entrants have the capability to meet the QTS standards by the end of their training and that they possess appropriate personal and intellectual qualities to be teachers;
- ensure that all entrants have achieved a standard equivalent to a grade C in the GCSE examination in English and mathematics;
- ensure that all entrants born on or after 1 September 1979 who enter primary or Key Stages 2/3 training have achieved a standard equivalent to a grade C in the GCSE examination in a science subject;
- ensure that all entrants have met the Secretary of State's requirements for physical and mental fitness to teach, as detailed in the relevant circular;
- ensure that systems are in place to seek information on whether entrants have a criminal background that might prevent them working with children or young persons, or as a teacher; and ensure that entrants have not previously been excluded from teaching or working with children;
- satisfy themselves that all entrants can read effectively, and are able to communicate clearly and accurately in spoken and written Standard English;
- ensure that, in the case of postgraduate courses of initial teacher training, entrants hold a degree of a UK higher education institution or equivalent qualification;
- ensure that, as part of the selection procedures, all candidates admitted for training have taken part in a group or individual interview. (TTA, 2002b: 14)

Many courses are over-subscribed, and every year lots of people who have expected to be on a training course by the following September are disappointed. Courses can set their own entry requirements that are higher than the TTA basic ones. The TTA runs taster courses around the country. Some of these are aimed at particular groups such as people from minority ethnic groups. These are well worth going to. They give you detailed information about routes into teaching, the answers to questions that you hadn't even thought of, organise meetings with teachers and time in schools, and enable you to meet people in the same boat.

In order to get QTS you have to train to teach two Key Stages, so the first thing you need to decide is which age group to opt for:

- Foundation stage and KS1: 3–7 year olds;
- KS1 and KS2: 5–11 year olds;
- KS2 and KS3: 7–14 year olds (not many courses for these Key Stages);
- KS3 and KS4: 11–16 year olds;
- KS4 and post-16: 14–19 year olds.

You need to decide whether you want to go for primary or secondary. The fundamental difference is that primary teachers teach the same class all subjects for the year whereas secondary teachers teach one subject to many different classes and year groups. Looking at your qualifications may help you decide. Degrees in a national curriculum subject are preferred for primary PGCEs, but if yours isn't it's not the end of the world – you'll just need to convince interviewers of its relevance. Primary course providers favour applicants who have a good range of National Curriculum subjects at GCSE and A level.

Secondary course providers like you to have a good degree in the subject you want to train to teach. Again, if things aren't that straightforward don't worry. You need to be at degree level in the subject you're getting qualified teacher status in by the *end* of the course, so you have time to get more knowledge on board. So, if your degree is in psychology but you want to teach maths for instance, you will need to emphasise how much maths there was in your course (statistics, etc) and how you have high grades in maths A level.

Routes to being a qualified teacher

Choosing the right route and course is essential. The TTA survey (2002d) of newly qualified teachers (NQTs) found that 85 per cent of secondary teachers rated their training as good or very good, though only 78 per cent of primary teachers did so. The rest were lukewarm. In fact, 2 per cent rated their training as poor. This is a small proportion and maybe they're the Moaning Myrtles for whom nothing can be good enough – but what if their courses really were that bad?

ICT and behaviour management continue to be areas identified as comparatively weak in training. Well, if you don't get good ICT training when you're at college you're unlikely to fare much better when you're in school! Even more worrying is that only 60 per cent of NQTs thought their courses prepared them to establish and maintain a good standard of discipline. I know much of this comes with experience, but it is a fundamental necessity.

Each institution sets its own entry requirements. Some will only take people with a 2.1 degree and all value classroom experience highly. Have a look at the Performance Profiles area of the TTA Web site (www.canteach.gov.uk/) to find out more about the institution you are considering. Look at the number of places available and their ratings from when they were inspected. Some institutions have many places. For instance, St Martin's College has 640 primary trainees and the Institute of Education has over 700 secondary PGCEs. At the opposite end of the scale, SCITTs (School-Centred Initial Teacher Training centres) often have fewer than 20 places.

Many people start training courses, but how many end up teaching? The TTA's Initial Teacher Training Performance Profiles (TTA, 2002e) are well worth looking at for this sort of information. Not everyone gets qualified teacher status at the end of training. Fifteen per cent of people doing primary and 22 per cent of people doing secondary maths PGCEs in London didn't get QTS. Maybe they dropped out, maybe they had to resit a teaching placement or maybe they failed. Someone on the *TES* New Teacher Forum posted this message:

From the **TES forum**

'Half of the muppets that get on courses are killing time after their degrees until they decide they can earn far more money in marketing/finance. I couldn't believe the half-hearted attitude of some people: lack of planning, subject knowledge, skiving lectures/school etc. It's a shame that people who are genuinely committed have to wait to get a place behind people like this who fancy the £6,000 training salary and another year at college.'

Of course, the $64,000 question is how many people actually go into teaching. Only 83 per cent of those who get QTS through primary PGCEs in London are teaching in the year after their course (TTA, 2002e) and this percentage includes those working abroad, in the independent sector and on supply. So, it looks as if for every 100 people who start a primary PGCE (Postgraduate Certificate in Education) in London only 85 qualify and 71 work as teachers. Similarly, for every 100 people who start a PGCE in secondary maths only 78 qualify and 69 end up teaching when they finish. Courses vary in their degree of drop out: look at the performance tables and choose somewhere that has a good track record.

The route you take through ITT (Initial Teacher Training), and the time it will take you to achieve QTS or Teaching Qualification (TQ) for Scotland, will depend on your circumstances. The QTS standards are the same whichever route you choose to go through, and all courses have to provide you with experience of at least two schools. There are three main routes to QTS, which are compared in Table 1.1:

- The undergraduate route – you combine subject studies with professional training over three or four years and get a BA (QTS) or a BEd.
- The postgraduate route – which is offered full time for one year, part-time or through a flexible programme and gives a Postgraduate Certificate in Education (PGCE) with QTS, unless the PGCE is for the post-compulsory (post-16 year old, eg, FE college) sector.

- Employment-based routes (England and Wales) – the Graduate Teacher Programme (GTP), which is for people with a degree, and the Registered Teacher Programme (RTP), which is small, and for people without a degree but with two years higher education such as an HND. Both courses give qualified teacher status. Be warned, Scotland doesn't recognise these routes.

	BEd, BA QTS	PGCE	GTP
Entry requirements	English and maths GCSE C, science C for primary students born after 1 September 1979	English and maths GCSE C, science C for primary students born after 1 September 1979; degree	English and maths GCSE C, science C for primary students born after 1 September 1979; degree; 24+
Apply through	UCAS	GTTR	TTA or a DRB
Time spent in school	Thirty-two weeks for four-year and twenty-four weeks for three-year courses	Twenty-four weeks for secondary and eighteen weeks for primary	Almost all
Funding	None	£6,000 bursary	£13,000 salary £4,000 training grant
£4,000 Golden Hello	No	Secondary maths, science, ICT, MFL, DT, English	No
Loans repaid	Secondary maths, science, ICT, MFL, DT, English	Secondary maths, science, ICT, MFL, DT, English	Secondary maths, science, ICT, MFL, DT, English
Numbers in secondary	1,313	15,472	3,400 secondary and primary
Numbers in primary	6,488	7,988	3,400 secondary and primary

Table 1.1   Comparing routes into teaching

Undergraduate route

The BA (QTS) or BEd is a teaching qualification and a degree, and takes three or four years. It's great for people who know that they really want to teach but is a bit limiting as a degree if you go into another career. Having said that, a degree is a degree and you will study at a high level in your specialist subject. Just under half of primary school trainees are on undergraduate courses, whereas the PGCE outnumbers the BA QTS/BEd by about 12:1 as you can see in Table 1.1. A constant irritant for people on undergraduate courses is that they aren't entitled to the £6,000 training bursary that their

PGCE colleagues get – and yet arguably have shown more commitment to teaching by doing a degree in education. Nor can they get the Golden Hello even if they teach a shortage subject, though they are entitled to have their student loans repaid. To choose a course, take a look at the UCAS Web site (www.ucas.co.uk), which holds information on all undergraduate courses available, but check out how they do in the TTA Performance Profiles too.

Postgraduate routes

You can apply for a place on a postgraduate course through the Graduate Teacher Training Registry (GTTR). The registry starts taking applications at the start of October and closes its books for primary courses in the middle of December, and at the end of June for secondary applications. The GTTR system is that you complete one form and state your training course preferences. Your form is sent to your first-choice institution and if it rejects you, it'll be sent to your second choice, and so on. Despite teacher shortages, it is not easy to get places on popular courses so it's best to apply in October rather than leaving it till later. Applications are processed by the GTTR in date of receipt order and dispatched to the institutions concerned on a weekly basis. You can see the progress of your application on the GTTR Web site (www.gttr.ac.uk).

PGCE

The PGCE is the most popular postgraduate route, and probably the safest in terms of ensuring that you get quality training. SCITTs and the GTP are more variable – some people have had great experiences and others have been neglected. PGCE courses last for about 38 weeks and are based at a university but involve a great deal of time in school, usually in six-week blocks. Primary PGCEs spend at least 18 weeks in school, and secondaries at least 24 weeks – over half of the course. When at college, you'll spend your time learning in lectures, seminars, workshops and tutorials. The PGCE combines theory and practice, in a way that your first degree may not have, and you will have written assignments to do as well as planning when you're in school. Take a look at the question posted to the New Teacher Forum Web site in the Top tip! box below.

Top tip!

Q: 'Can you apply for a PGCE before you have finished your degree so you have a place ready for September? Are places conditional on getting a certain class of degree? Also, is there any restriction on having school experience or can you get on a course without any?'

A: Yes, lots of people apply for a PGCE in the last year of their degree. Any offer will be conditional on you passing your degree, and some courses may expect you to get a 2.2 or a 2.1. University references often say what sort of grades you've been given so far and some predict what class of degree you'll get. You're unlikely to get a PGCE place without having some recent experience of schools (other than having been a pupil!) so get out to at least one for the equivalent of about a week to see what teaching is really like. Then you'll know whether you really want to teach, and have something to talk about in the interview.

Fast Track

The Fast Track programme is for a small number of people who do a PGCE at specified institutions. It aims to be an accelerated development programme towards leadership positions. You'll be given a laptop and some other items and are expected to attend a few extra sessions. When working you'll get an extra point on your salary, which is funded by the DfES. To find out more about the Fast Track programme go to www.fasttrackteaching.gov.uk but beware, the entry requirements are high. You need a strong academic record. You will need a 2.1 degree, or a 2.2 plus a postgraduate degree, eg, MA, MSc, PhD, etc in a relevant subject. You'll also need either 22 UCAS points in subjects excluding General Studies (using the old points tariff, ie, an A=10 points, B=8, C=6, D=4, E=2), or at least two of the following:

- eighteen UCAS points (excluding General Studies);
- a postgraduate degree in a discipline relevant to the subject you want to teach (this option cannot be used if you have a 2.2 degree);
- a professional qualification that is relevant to the subject you want to teach;

- three years' work experience in a graduate or professional role that is relevant to the subject you want to teach.

The selection procedures are gruelling. If your application form shows that you meet the academic entry requirements, you'll have:

- a half-day computer-based assessment;
- an interview for a PGCE;
- a two-day residential assessment, where your potential to succeed on the Fast Track programme will be tested thoroughly.

The other downside is that you can't apply to standard adverts. There is a system of job brokering so that you work in schools that have recruited for a Fast Track position. You'll be expected to move posts every two to three years.

Flexible routes

If you aren't able to train full time on a traditional postgraduate course you might be interested in a flexible programme. Courses have multiple start and finish dates. Some have modules that you can do in the evening or weekends, via distance-learning packages, others have an intensive full-time programme over a short time. At the start of your training, your previous achievement and learning will be assessed. This will be used to design a training and assessment programme that meets your individual needs. During your training you will receive support and guidance on your progress from the Higher Education Institution and schools involved in your training.

SCITT

School-Centred Initial Teacher Training (SCITT) is run by groups of schools, with input from higher education institutions and Local Education Authorities. All courses lead to Qualified Teacher Status upon successful completion and may also lead to a PGCE validated by an HE institution. You will spend almost all your time in schools. There are a fair number of SCITTs, but each has only a small number of places.

Employment-based routes

GTP

The Graduate Teacher Programme (GTP) is for people with a first degree who want to train on the job in England or Wales. However, Scotland doesn't recognise it as a teaching qualification. It suits people who have already got a good amount of school experience already, because it can take only one, two or three terms, depending on your needs. Entry is competitive, with places going to the best applications in priority funding categories, which are:

1. secondary shortage subjects – mathematics, science, modern foreign languages, ICT, DT and English;
2. high quality primary applications;
3. applications in any subject or phase that make the teaching force more representative of society, for example increasing the number of men in primary teaching, teachers from minority ethnic groups and teachers with disabilities;
4. high quality secondary applications in any subject;
5. applications to train people currently working as teaching assistants.

The TTA pays a grant of up to £4,000 to cover the cost of training and may pay up to £13,000 to the school as a contribution to the trainee's salary. This is subject to tax and national insurance.

The snag with the GTP is that you have to start working in a school as a teacher before even applying. Places are very competitive and experiences have been mixed, with a fair number of people feeling that they were left to sink or swim. At the end you'll just have QTS, not a PGCE, so there is a slightly lower status. On the positive side you probably won't have to go to lectures or write essays.

> **From the TES forum**
>
> 'I've been doing the GTP for about six months now. To be quite honest, don't do it to yourself! I have a 90 per cent timetable, am responsible for all the planning, marking, assessment to teach secondary English to KS3 and 4 with very little support within the department. Yes, it is fantastic to have your own class but do you need the added stress while you're still learning? My average week is: arrive at school 7 am, leave 6 pm. Home to dinner (my husband makes it while I'm marking) and then I work till about 11 pm. Saturday is like any other school day except I work at home. The PGCE course is hard enough but to teach full time, be totally responsible for the classes, while effectively doing a university course in your spare time is impossible.'

If you trained to be a teacher overseas

Unless people are qualified to teach in a country that is part of the European Economic Area, they will need to get QTS here in order to be classed as fully qualified – and be paid accordingly. Overseas trained teachers (OTTs) do not need to be qualified here in order to work – they can teach for four years without QTS and many are understandably resentful when they realise that the qualification from their own country does not fully qualify them to teach in England. However, in my experience, people become more effective teachers in English schools through gaining QTS, and it gives them a focus for their professional development, the possibility of passing the Threshold – and another qualification for the CV. Another incentive is that they can be assessed for exemption from induction (TTA, 2003a) at the same time as for QTS, if they have been teaching for more than two years in this country or elsewhere.

If you're an OTT, remember that there is much more to getting QTS than being a good teacher. It can be a long process unless you know the system. The initial step is to contact the OTT Advice Line (01245 454321) who will send you a pack of useful materials and the application form. *How to Qualify as a Teacher in England* (TTA, 2003a) contains everything you need to know, but needs very careful reading.

The first thing to check is qualifications. The TTA insists that all people applying for QTS need to provide their *original* – not photo-copied – proof of degree and GCSE equivalent qualifications. Degrees from other countries are not always equivalent. The National Academic Recognition Information Centre (NARIC 01242 260010) can provide information on the comparability of overseas qualifications to UK qualifications and the OTT Advice Line and universities can check qualifications on the NARIC database.

The application form is an off-putting 26 pages long! Before you start filling it in, get some expert advice. The TTA gives schools vouchers for experts to do advisory visits to explain the procedures and advise on options. The OTT Advice Line organises these on request from a school. The person carrying out the advisory visit will explain the:

- standards for Qualified Teacher Status;
- induction standards and pros and cons of applying for exemption from induction if the teacher has two years' experience;
- assessment process;
- skills tests in literacy, numeracy and ICT that have to be taken online at designated centres.

You may want someone from an RB (Recommending Body) or teacher training institution who knows the QTS and induction regulations well and who can audit you against the standards and suggest ways to address gaps in your knowledge, experience and skills. The OTT information pack contains a list of RBs (larger university-type institutions can be termed DRBs or Designated Recommending Bodies). They take responsibility for ensuring that the application is completed correctly – the TTA has to query about half of the forms at the moment. Alternatively, your school can be the RB if you have members of staff who are very familiar with the QTS and induction standards and regulations – and who have time to audit, train and mentor you. Otherwise, you risk having to field time-consuming queries about your application form and risk failing the assessment, through not being prepared fully.

The assessment is in two parts. Like anyone training to be a teacher, OTTs have to meet all the standards for QTS, including the skills tests in numeracy, literacy and ICT before they can be awarded QTS. Once applications have been approved, OTTs are sent a registration number and can apply to take the tests at one of the designated centres. There is more information about the skills tests in Chapter 2.

The main assessment takes place in school and is carried out by an assessor for a day and a half (or two days for induction and QTS). During this time, OTTs have to *demonstrate* that they meet the standards. Being a good teacher is not enough. The assessor will need evidence of the knowledge and teaching experience in two consecutive Key Stages. There are three sorts of evidence (see the standards for the award of QTS status, Chapter 2):

- documentation – CV, planning, assessment, reports, notes from observations carried out by others, pupils' work from two Key Stages, etc;
- observation of teaching – a minimum of two hours for QTS only and three hours for QTS plus exemption from induction;
- discussion with the OTT and others who know his or her work.

Financial incentives

Think about the financial incentives when considering whether to do an undergraduate or postgraduate teacher training course, whether to go for primary or secondary, and what subject to go for. There are three sorts of financial incentives:

- the training bursary;
- Golden Hellos;
- Repayment of Teacher Loans.

The training bursary

People doing undergraduate courses get no training bursary, though if you do a PGCE in England or Wales you'll get £6,000. Your training institution pays this to you, usually from October in 9 or 10 lots. Schools with people on the GTP are eligible for £13,000 to contribute to a training salary (taxed) and £4,000 to cover the costs of their training. However, because there is a limited budget some people get only the training grant or not even that. The school funds it entirely.

Golden Hellos

You can claim the £4,000 Golden Hello in England and Wales if you're taking a PGCE in secondary maths, science, English, modern foreign languages, design & technology or information & communications technology; the same subjects apply in Wales, with the addition of Welsh. You can only claim the money when you've successfully completed induction and are still teaching that shortage subject in a maintained school. There is more information about Golden Hellos in Chapter 5.

Repayment of Teacher Loans (RTL) scheme

Any loans taken out with the Student Loans Company will be paid off, by the government via the RTL scheme, over 10 years for full-time teachers with income contingent loans, or around five to seven years for those with older mortgage-style loans. However, this is only for people who teach maths, science, modern foreign languages, English (including drama), Welsh, design & technology, or ICT for at least half of their teaching time in a normal week. It's open to people working in maintained schools, non-maintained special schools, City Technology Colleges (CTC), City Colleges for the Technology of the Arts, and City Academies in England and Wales. In this respect, the RTL is much fairer than the Golden Hello, which is limited to those with PGCEs and excludes people in CTCs and City Academies. The only people who are excluded are those working in independent schools – there are even deals for people in Further Education colleges. There is more information on the RTL scheme in Chapter 5.

Primary teachers are only eligible if they teach shortage subjects to classes other than their own and do so for half the week. This is clearly unfair – primary schools aren't organised like that. So, in practice, the RTL is unlikely to be an option for many in the primary sector. However, I do know one person who will get her £17,000 loan repaid. She has a Year 5 class and teaches Year 5 and 6 sets in English, maths and science every morning.

So, if you're torn between say primary and secondary English, secondary art & design or design & technology, or maths and business studies, it would be financially beneficial to consider the implications of the incentive schemes. For more information go to the TTA Web site or ring its Teaching Information Line on 0845 6000991 (6000992 for Welsh speakers) or, for the RTL Helpline at the Student Loans Company, 0870 240 6298.

The application form

As soon as you've decided what route you want to go down and which course to apply for, you need to sit down with the application form. Some institutions get more than five applications for every place they have so they weed many people out from their form. Yours needs to be good. Here are some tips:

- As soon as you get your application form, photocopy it. Draft a rough copy before you complete the real form.
- Read through it to see the information it requires.
- Check the closing date and make sure that you have plenty of time to contact referees, draft the form, write the personal statement, complete the form, check it and post it.
- How many referees does it ask for? Normally you need to name two, though only the first may be used. Choose people who can say good things about your academic work and any experience working in schools or, failing that, with young people. Remember to ask people if it is okay for you to put their names as referees and let them know time frames.
- List your work experience clearly, emphasising things that are related to teaching. Follow any instructions about sending photocopies or SAE, using black ink and deadlines (these will be stuck to).
- Write down all your qualifications, dates and grades – for instance, even if you failed GCSE biology at least it will be useful to know that you studied it until you were 16.

- If you have yet to take or get the results of any qualifications, make this clear. This is particularly true for people retaking maths, science or English GCSE.
- Don't leave any box empty. For instance, people may assume that you have only a Pass degree or a Third if you don't write in the grade of degree.
- Write neatly, don't make any errors, use a black pen and make sure it doesn't smudge!

Your personal statement

Your personal statement needs to say why you want to be a teacher and why you should be given a place on the course. The reader will have to decide whether your application merits you being interviewed. You have limited space to write so you'll need to plan what you say with great care so that you cover all the main points. Remember that the reader wants to be able to tell that you:

- will be able to meet the QTS standards – so they'll choose people who are well on the way to doing so, especially in terms of subject knowledge. A broad range of national curriculum subjects at GCSE and A level will go some way to compensating for a non-national curriculum degree subject.
- have the personal and intellectual capacity to be a teacher. You need to show intelligence and that you get on well with adults and children.
- can read effectively. So do everything the application instructions require!
- communicate clearly and accurately in English. Take great care with your grammar, punctuation and spelling, and construct your writing concisely and as well as possible. I cannot tell you how many appalling howlers or illegible personal statements I have come across. Do not fall at this first and very straightforward fence.
- are committed to working with young people, particularly as a teacher. The role of a playscheme worker is different to that of a teacher.
- have a good understanding of what teaching in schools nowadays involves. Say exactly what recent experience you have

had in schools and, if necessary, what you have arranged to have. If this isn't evident somewhere on the form you will probably be rejected.

- are committed to doing a teaching course. There is a high drop-out rate, so the person sifting through the applications will be looking for evidence of enthusiasm and staying power.

You also want your personal statement to be personal. Avoid blanket assertions but give examples of what you've done, especially in schools: 'Observing in two schools has broadened my understanding of the importance of thorough planning to meet the needs of all children – and the time and expertise that this requires.'

When structuring your writing think of how to be helpful to the reader. Express yourself with care. Address any problematic issues (poor qualifications, gaps in employment) that the reader is likely to have picked up in reading the information parts of the application form. Try to turn things to advantage.

Finally, keep a photocopy and read it again just before your interview. Get into a school so that you can speak about a recent experience at interview. You'll only get about two weeks' notice of the interview, which will probably last half a day.

Interviews

You've been offered an interview – how exciting, but how terrifying! Again, preparation will be the key. Plan your journey with care, leaving room for the unexpected. There's nothing that looks so bad as being late for an interview. Web sites such as http://journeyplanner.tfl.gov.uk/ are invaluable.

What to wear? You've got to feel good, and look the part. Your appearance will have an effect, possibly subconscious and therefore all the more powerful. Research shows that the content of what you say is only part of the impact that you make on interviewers. Voice and appearance matter hugely. Wear smart clothes, but make sure you'll be comfortable. Shoes can be a real problem if you're on your feet all day. A reasonably conservative look is safe but jazz it up with interesting jewellery or a tie to express your personality. Smell is important, too – don't turn up reeking of cigarettes or strong scent. And remember that there is nothing worse than a rumbling belly or a jolly ring-tone when you're trying to impress.

Take a file with your application form, the prospectus, the letter detailing the interview schedule and a copy of the most recent *Times Educational Supplement* (*TES*). You can read this while waiting. It will make you look professional, switch your brain into education mode, and may come in handy in answering a question or two.

Possible interview formats

Interviews vary in how they are structured and how long they last. These would be questions to ask when you phone to accept the interview, if the information isn't outlined in the letter. Here's one institution's interview structure for a place on a primary PGCE. Each activity takes up to half an hour:

1. Introductory talk about the course and opportunity for questions.
2. Group activity – watch a video of part of a lesson then discuss it in threes with someone watching and assessing you. This will be assessing your interpersonal skills, so don't dominate or be a wall flower and remember body language.
3. Numeracy test – interpreting data, similar to one of the numeracy skills test activities.
4. Literacy test – correcting a badly written letter.
5. Individual interview.

What are your interviewers looking for? Commitment, a realistic understanding of what teaching is like; someone who acts, dresses and speaks professionally, someone who is going to be successful on the course, that is, can write well, is punctual, can cope with pressure, appears to like children, is intelligent, can work in a team, has good subject knowledge, and takes care with presentation. That's all!!

Top tip!

Q: 'I've been asked to give a 10-minute presentation on an activity carried out within a school environment...'

A: Talk about some teaching and learning that you have seen, what you liked about it, what the children learned (focus on one or two), what the teacher did to make it happen. If you haven't been in a class recently get into one quick – you can't do it without.

In the presentation be lively, engage your audience, have some visual aids (children's work) and most of all come across as reflective. Could the children have learned more? How could the teacher have done it even better? Don't come across as overly critical. Plan and rehearse it well so that you keep to your 10-minute slot.

Interview tips

- Relax. I know it's hard but breathe deeply, wriggle your toes or do whatever works for you.
- Consider questions before answering and don't be frightened of a few seconds' silence – it's better than gabbling nervously.
- Be reflective.
- Make eye contact with whoever is asking you a question.
- If you're stumped on a question, smile and ask them to repeat the question.
- Be enthusiastic.

You're likely to be asked questions along these lines:

- Why do you want a place on this course and for this phase?
- Why have you chosen this subject/age phase?
- What are the current issues in (eg, history) education and teaching?
- Why is your subject (eg, history) important?
- Justify the relevance of your degree to the teaching you'll be doing.
- What makes a good classroom?
- How would you handle some difficult behaviour?

- Describe how you would spend a typical day if you were a teacher.
- How would you ensure that all children were treated equally in your class? Bear in mind gender, race, academic ability and language acquisition.
- What role should parents play in education?
- How will you exploit opportunities for literacy and numeracy in your subject?
- What areas of subject knowledge are you weaker on and how do you plan to remedy them?
- Tell us about a current educational issue and your views on it.
- What do you think the most challenging part of the course will be?
- What skills will you bring to teaching?
- What experience have you had that could help in your teaching career?
- Do you have any questions? You have, because you are an intelligent person who wants to look highly committed. How about drop-out rate or employment chances from the course?

Answers to that hardest question of all, 'Why do you want to be a teacher?', might include one or more of the following:

- A teacher inspired me when I was a child.
- It's fun, varied. I'll never look at the clock.
- I like children.
- I want to do a worthwhile job.
- I like the creativity.
- I love my subject, and want to pass on my passion.
- The holidays will fit in with my family commitments.
- I want to give something back to society.
- I enjoy acting.
- Teaching is a profession that values professional development.
- I won't just be making money for someone else.

Or maybe you don't feel any of these, in which case maybe you should try another career!

Justifying your degree can be hard, even when it should be easy. For instance, your English Literature degree will be relevant to your work as a primary school teacher because... er... What do you think of these reasons:

> English is the medium by which almost all learning takes place, so children need good levels of literacy to help them learn in all subjects. The knowledge gained in my degree will therefore be used throughout the curriculum, but it will be of particular use in teaching literacy. I am very widely read. This will be useful in choosing texts. I can analyse texts well and have a deep understanding of terms such as metaphor, homophone, and alliteration. I write and speak well, and can explain how different uses of grammar affect meaning, for instance. Perhaps most importantly, I have a love of stories, plays and poetry that I hope to convey to the children, and which will turn them into avid readers and keen writers.

Once you get on a course you will need to meet the standards for qualified teacher status. The standards and the skills tests are outlined in the next chapter.

two

What you have to do to get QTS

> The standards for the award of Qualified Teacher Status
>
> The skills tests

The standards for the award of Qualified Teacher Status

The standards for the award of Qualified Teacher Status in England (TTA, 2002b) set out what you must know, understand and be able to do to be awarded QTS. They apply to all trainee teachers, whatever route or course they're on. The standards are organised in three interrelated sections:

1. Professional Values and Practice.
2. Knowledge and Understanding.
3. Teaching – this section is broken down into three parts, which are underpinned by the values and knowledge covered in the first two sections:
   - Planning;
   - Monitoring and Assessment;
   - Teaching and Class Management.

Here are the Professional Values and Practice standards to give you a flavour of what is expected. The rest of the QTS standards are in Appendix 1.

Professional Values and Practice
Those awarded Qualified Teacher Status must understand and

uphold the professional code of the General Teaching Council for England by demonstrating all of the following:

1.1 They have high expectations of all pupils; respect their social, cultural, linguistic, religious and ethnic backgrounds; and are committed to raising their educational achievement.

1.2 They treat pupils consistently, with respect and consideration, and are concerned for their development as learners.

1.3 They demonstrate and promote the positive values, attitudes and behaviour that they expect from their pupils.

1.4 They can communicate sensitively and effectively with parents and carers, recognising their roles in pupils' learning, and their rights, responsibilities and interests in this.

1.5 They can contribute to, and share responsibly in, the corporate life of schools.

1.6 They understand the contribution that support staff and other professionals make to teaching and learning.

1.7 They are able to improve their own teaching, by evaluating it, learning from the effective practice of others and from evidence. They are motivated and able to take increasing responsibility for their own professional development.

1.8 They are aware of, and work within, the statutory frameworks relating to teachers' responsibilities.

These sound quite easy but each standard covers a huge area. For instance 1.8 covers school teachers' pay and conditions (DfES, 2002a) and all their legal responsibilities – both massive and important areas. So, when looking at the standards be aware that there are degrees to which they can be achieved, and find out what's expected of you for QTS.

The evidence that you're meeting standards comes in three forms. The acronym DOD is useful to remember:

- **d**ocumentation: written evidence such as planning, assessment, marking and essays;
- **o**bservation: observations of you in the classroom;
- **d**iscussion: discussion with you and people who know your work.

The *Handbook of Guidance* (TTA, 2002c) is useful in explaining exactly what is expected for each standard. The guidance is organised under three headings:

- Scope – how much you have to know about in this area;
- Evidence Relevant to Meeting the Standard – the sort of thing that you should be doing;
- Further References – a useful list of key documents.

For instance Standard 2.6 on Special Educational Needs (SEN) says that you must demonstrate that you understand your responsibilities under the *SEN Code of Practice*, and know how to seek advice from specialists on less common types of special educational needs. The TTA guidance is given in more detail in the boxed text below.

TTA guidance on SEN

Scope (TTA, 2002c: 49)

Teachers' classes are likely to consist of pupils with a range of ability, including those who have special educational needs and disabilities. For some pupils, special arrangements may be made to enable them to overcome barriers to learning, have full access to the curriculum, and remain full members of the teacher's class. This Standard requires trainees to be aware of their responsibilities, the legislative requirements relating to SEN and disability, and the rationale for the inclusion of those with special educational needs and disabilities in mainstream education. This will involve an understanding of the graduated framework of identification, assessment and intervention set out in the *SEN Code of Practice*; the kinds of provision that might be made through school action, school action plus, or through a statement of special educational needs; and the role of the class or subject teacher within this framework.

In order to seek advice, trainees will need to be aware of the role of the Special Education Needs Coordinator (SENCO), and how an Individual Education Plan (IEP) is used as a planning and teaching tool. Trainees should know how to access the advice they need to support the learning needs of pupils with SEN and disabilities, and be aware of the sources of advice likely to be available to them outside the school – for example, via the Internet, from LEA SEN support services, special schools, health professionals and voluntary organisations. Trainees will not be expected to have the same level of expertise as experienced teachers or the SENCO, or to draw up an IEP independently. Trainees should understand that a pupil with a disability or a medical condition or diagnosis may not necessarily have SEN as defined by law. Having English as an additional language (EAL) is not a special educational need.

Evidence Relevant to Meeting the Standard
Trainees' knowledge of pupils with SEN and disabilities will come mainly from their work in schools, although other training activities could be used to supplement this. School-based evidence could include how trainees' plans take account of any pupils in the class with IEPs or their teaching of specific pupils with special educational needs, with or without the support of specialist staff. Trainees may also demonstrate their knowledge through discussion with tutors or a school's SENCO, contributing to school-based in-service training, or through responding to a case study of a child with special educational needs, showing that they are aware of the need to do this in confidence and with tact.

Further References
DfES (2001) *SEN Code of Practice*, and the accompanying SEN toolkit.
Disability Discrimination Act (1995) Part IV.
Education Act (1996) Part IV.
QCA (2001) *Guidelines for Planning, Teaching and Assessing the Curriculum for Pupils with Learning Difficulties.*

Each standard has a useful list of other relevant standards to help you cross-reference. For instance, Standard 3.3.9 on managing behaviour, that those with QTS should 'set high expectations for pupils' behaviour and establish a clear framework for classroom discipline to anticipate and manage pupils' behaviour constructively, and promote self-control and independence', is related to S2.7 on knowledge of strategies to promote good behaviour, S1.2 (treating pupils consistently), S1.3 (demonstrating the behaviour teachers expect from pupils), S3.2.2 (giving constructive feedback), S3.2.4 (supporting pupils with difficulties), S3.3.1 (building successful relationships), S3.3.3 (interesting and motivating pupils) and S3.3.14 (challenging bullying or harassment).

Accreditation of prior learning

People can be accredited for their prior learning and experience. This may mean that there are parts of the course that you won't need to do in such depth, so that you can spend more time addressing things that you're not so good at. Your trainers will be looking at whether you are well on the way to meeting any of the QTS standards before the course as a result of your experience. The difficulty lies in that there are gradations of meeting any criteria – you can always know more and do things even better.

If you feel that you already have a great deal of knowledge and experience, get a folder and organise evidence such as your CV and job descriptions around each of the standards. For instance, Standard 1.2 that teachers should 'treat pupils consistently, with respect and consideration, and are concerned for their development as learners' is something you would consider you've done if you've worked as a classroom assistant. Evidence could come from you citing some examples that could be backed up with the signature of someone who you've worked for. Think of all the little things you've done, the way you spoke that showed that you treat children with respect and consideration.

However, don't exaggerate what you know and can do – there's nothing to be gained. You want to be as good a teacher as you can by the end of your training, and repeating or going deeper into things can be really beneficial.

The skills tests

In order to meet Standard 2.8 all trainee teachers must pass the skills tests in ICT, literacy and numeracy, irrespective of their qualifications, subject specialisation or age group taught. They were brought in in 2001 amid great controversy. The Teacher Training Agency's reason for inventing them is 'to ensure everyone qualifying to teach has a good grounding in the use of numeracy, literacy and ICT in the wider context of their professional role as a teacher' (TTA, 2002d). Fine, but it's pretty insulting to think that these things wouldn't be picked up easily in the course of training by graduates who have to have maths and English GCSE – and why have a test for these things? Would you ever have to work out this little gem from the mental arithmetic part of the numeracy test in test conditions?

> A teacher started an activity that lasted 1¼ hours at 13.35. What time did the activity finish?

The problems are meant to be about the professional role of a teacher but there are questions such as:

> Geography maps cost £3 each for the first 20 purchased and £2.70 for each additional map. What was the cost of purchasing 22 maps?

Ordering equipment is meant to be one of the 25 common tasks that the DfES says teachers should delegate to support staff. So much for joined-up thinking. Typical comments from people on the Web Forum who have done them are included in the Inbox below.

⌨ *From the* **TES forum**

'They were basic and easy to do, and the whole process was well organised, but they were hyped up to be a lot worse than they were. It was too much added stress for nothing.'

'They are an extra hassle in an already horrifically busy schedule. The fact that we need GCSE English, maths and science to get on the course should be enough evidence without these tests.'

'I passed the tests, but they were a waste of time. I should have been concentrating on my teaching practice.'

Still, everyone needs to pass all three skills tests in order to get QTS. Don't allow yourself to worry about them until you've failed at least one, if not two, attempts. I know that's no comfort to those of you who go to pieces in tests, don't feel very confident at maths/literacy/ICT, aren't brilliant with computers, especially an unfamiliar one, and would prefer to be tested with a pencil and paper. Put them into perspective. Surely compared to teaching 30 children every day, they should be seen as a minor inconvenience? I hope this chapter will reassure you that they're perfectly doable: to be forewarned is to be forearmed.

Registering and booking

When I said 'minor inconvenience' I was referring to the tests themselves. Registering and booking them have been challenges in themselves for many people. It's all quite a palaver. Before booking your test you must register using the seven-digit registration number that will be given to you from your training provider (or direct from the TTA if you're on the GTP, RTP or OTT), and enter candidate information. You're asked for details of your place of birth, training provider, date of birth, gender, ethnic group, type of training course, areas of specialism, when you expect to be recommended for the award of QTS, whether English is your first language and whether you will be requiring special arrangements within the tests...

> ### From the *TES forum*
> '...and whether you'd like an alarm call and your eggs runny or hard. OK, I made the last two up. But, assuming the TTA had a vague idea of who we were before deciding to issue us with a personalised registration number, that seems 10 steps more than is necessary.' David Ogle, *TES*, 20 November 2001

If you have a disability such as dyslexia or a visual or hearing impairment, or if English is not your first language, you can apply for 25 per cent additional time in which to complete the test. This is well worth going for, but can only be done at the time of registering.

Once you've registered, you will receive a username and password by e-mail to the address provided during registration within two working days. These are used to actually book the tests.

From the **TES forum**
'The cynical among us reckoned that having got through this process we had automatically passed our ICT skills test. We were wrong.'

Book the tests as soon as you can. The tests are taken online at designated centres throughout the country. It's important to book these up in plenty of time, to allow time to resit before the end of your course. Details of directions, maps and general opening hours for each test centre are on the TTA Web site. When you've chosen a centre you book a test online. You can only book one test at a time but you may as well book to take all three tests on the same day. The literacy and numeracy tests run for 45 and 48 minutes respectively and the ICT test takes 35 minutes. Allow yourself time to take a quick break between tests – for example, numeracy test booked for 9 am; ICT booked for 11 am; literacy booked for 12 am. Then off for a nice spot of lunch!

When you take the tests you must have photographic proof of identity. The only equipment you'll need is a pen or pencil. Paper for rough working out and an on-screen calculator is provided. You will get your results at the end of the test.

Prepare

You need to prepare for the skills tests, as you would any other exam. I've known people who've come a cropper because they thought that because they had a degree in the subject that they would be okay. So some preparation is needed but don't go overboard – you can take them as many times as you need and no one will know that you didn't pass first time unless you tell them. Support materials on the TTA Web site help you practise sample questions, test yourself, check your answers and consult the commentary provided on the questions. There are interactive and non-interactive practice tests. The benchmark tests are useful. They help you get a feel for the level of knowledge required to pass the tests. Look at the pass mark for these benchmark tests – at 60 per cent, this equates to 26 out of 43 marks for the literacy test; 17 out of 28 marks for the numeracy test and 26 out of 43 marks for the ICT test. There are also books on the market. Of vital importance is that you get used to working quickly, since the tests have a time limit. More information is available from the TTA Web site at http://www.tta.gov.uk/training/skillstests/.

Most people say they find the literacy test easiest. This is reinforced by the *Report on National Results* data (TTA, 2002d), which looked just at the literacy and numeracy tests. Table 2.1 shows that although the overall pass rates in 2001 on both the numeracy and literacy tests were high, trainees often needed more attempts to pass numeracy than literacy. Table 2.2 gives the mean number of attempts needed to pass, for all trainees and for certain sub-groups. Undergraduate trainees needed slightly more attempts than postgraduates, and people training to teach the 3–8 age group took more attempts than those training to teach older primary pupils. People whose first language is not English needed more attempts in both tests than the average.

	Pass at first try	Pass at second try	All attempts
Numeracy	81%	92%	98%
Literacy	90%	96%	99%

Table 2.1   How many people pass on the first and subsequent attempts (TTA, 2002d)

	Overall mean number of attempts needed to pass	
	Numeracy	Literacy
All trainees	1.28	1.14
Female	1.32	1.12
Male	1.14	1.20
Undergraduate courses	1.34	1.16
Postgraduate courses	1.25	1.13
Overseas trained teachers	1.21	1.24
Employment-based routes	1.28	1.16
English as first language	1.26	1.13
English not first language	1.55	1.35

Table 2.2   Number of attempts to pass (TTA, 2002d)

Numeracy test

Each numeracy test covers:

- mental arithmetic (12 marks);
- interpreting and using statistical information (7 marks);
- using and applying general arithmetic (9 marks).

Most people find the mental arithmetic hardest, but again practice helps. You have to wear headphones, then questions such as the ones in Figure 2.1 are read aloud.

From the *TES forum*

'The maths is an oddity. The mental maths bit is weird, because you listen and get two goes at it, but once the question is gone, it's gone. BUT you don't have to get them all right to pass, so if you missed one, or two, it's OK.'

'On the mental maths they read the question twice. Write the key numbers first time and listen the second.'

Literacy test

Each literacy test covers four areas:

- spelling (10 marks available);
- grammar (8–12 marks available);
- punctuation (15 marks available);
- comprehension (8–12 marks available).

Spelling must be attempted first and then the other three sections may be attempted in any order. In the spelling test you're asked to write words that you hear but they are put into the context of some sentences about school. The TTA chooses words that aren't unusual but which are a little tricky, such as accommodation, receipt, available, initiative, advertisement, strategies. In the punctuation test, the little hand turns grey when it is expecting you to insert a change. It won't let you put a piece of punctuation where none should be.

Q. No	Question
1	Geography maps cost £3 each for the first 20 purchased and £2.70 for each additional map. What was the cost of purchasing 22 maps?
2	In a test a pupil scored 18 marks out of 25. What was the pupil's score as a percentage?
3	A teacher taught GCSE science to three classes of 24 pupils and two classes of 27 pupils. Each of these pupils needed a textbook. How many textbooks were needed?
4	On a school exchange to Belgium, a group of pupils travelled 85 miles. Using the conversion of 5 miles being equal to 8 kilometres, how many kilometres did they travel?
5	Results showed that in Class A, 79% of boys achieved Level 4 and above. In Class B, 15 out of 20 boys achieved this standard. What was the difference between the two classes in the percentage of boys achieving Level 4 and above?
6	For a school play, 120 tickets were sold at £1.50 each and a further 100 child tickets were sold at 75 pence each. What was the total amount of money raised from ticket sales?
7	As part of a $2\frac{1}{2}$-hour literature workshop, pupils watched a film lasting 1 hour and 42 minutes. How many minutes of the workshop remained?
8	Last year a colour printer cost £180. This year the cost has increased by 5%. How much does the printer cost this year?
9	What is 6.03 multiplied by 100?
10	A test had 50 questions worth 1 mark each. The pass mark was 60%. How many questions had to be answered correctly to pass the test?
11	In a class of 28 pupils, 3/7 were boys. How many boys were there in the class?
12	A teacher started an activity that lasted $1\frac{1}{4}$ hours at 13.35. What time did the activity finish? Give your answer using the 24-hour clock.

Figure 2.1   Mental maths example (http://www.tta.gov.uk/ training/skillstests/)

Here is an example of the punctuation test:

Most of the original punctuation has been removed from the following passage:

.	,	:	;	?	-	'	'	'	'	'	( )	new paragraph
A	B	C	D	E	F	G	H	I	J	K	L	M	N	O	P	Q	R	S	T	U	V	W	X	Y	Z

What should teachers and parents be aware of

The Internet is a reflection of the people who make up our society it is not controlled by any particular organisation and the standard or source of information cannot always be guaranteed. Individuals rights to freedom of speech and freedom of choice must be observed, but balanced against the rights of younger users although not common users will also wish to guard against the possibility of 'hacking' and computer viruses.

While schools and parents need to exercise caution in the access which they allow children to the Internet they should not be deterred from using it its educational benefits outweigh any possible dangers, which are comparatively minimal. Schools have always helped learners to engage with society through clear support and guidance, and use of the Internet should be no exception.

As with television and video parents carers and teachers should preview material or provide supervision, as well as having a more general strategy in place for ensuring childrens safe use of the Internet. These strategies can use a combination of measures (http://www.tta.gov.uk/training/skillstests/)

The comprehension test involves reading several paragraphs, then answering some multiple-choice questions. The grammar is fairly straightforward. You're asked to select the best of some given alternatives at the points at which there are blank lines in a memo from a class tutor recommending a pupil for a commendation certificate to a Head of Year, for instance. You need to check that you have made the best overall set of choices for completing the passage, which might read, for example:

I suggest Abdul Rashid for a commendation certificate. Abdul's successes this half-term include:

- being consistently on time for registration;
- completes homework and hands it in promptly;
- completing and handing in promptly his homework;
- completing homework and handing it in promptly;
- acting as homework monitor for Ms Saheed.

As monitor he also checked for latecomers and made sure that the last of the books was handed in.
    In addition, Abdul has been responsible for helping the lunch time assistants.
    Finally,

- having been very negative in the past, his change of attitude has been most encouraging this term.
- Abdul's attitude, having been very negative in the past, has been most encouraging this term.

- having been very negative in the past, Abdul has been most encouraging this term.
- his attitude has been most encouraging this term. Having been very negative in the past.
  (http://www.tta.gov.uk/training/skillstests/)

ICT test

Each ICT test covers a balance of the following specific skills:

- researching and categorising information;
- developing and modelling information;
- presenting and communicating information.

To do so it covers your knowledge of the following types of software:

- word processor;
- spreadsheet;
- database;
- presentation;
- e-mail;
- Web browser.

It's a bit like testing you on everything in Microsoft Office but with some irritating differences. The spreadsheet is like Excel but it doesn't have the handy icons. Instead, there are words that you have to scroll down. Just keep calm and work through slowly.

From the *TES forum*

'Forget everything you know about computers. They have devised their own system for you to do the test on. Download the test from the Web site and practise. That way you'll be fine. A chappie on my course only did three out of the four tasks, and he passed!!!!'

All the files that you need for the test are in the 'Desktop folder'. Web sites that need to be accessed can be found in the bookmarks section of your 'Web browser' and e-mail addresses can be found in the address book section of your 'E-mail'. Other comments from the Forum include:

> ### From the *TES forum*
>
> 'I think the hardest bit was putting information from the e-mail address book into word documents and vice versa, I didn't expect that!'
>
> 'The ICT task is practically all there on screen. For instance if the test is asking you to add a field to a database, the instructions at the top of the program have "add field".'
>
> 'You can't right click during the test.'
>
> 'I had to restart one section as I was trying to do something by trial and error and ended up making a big error that I could not fix!'
>
> 'I downloaded the ICT practice test from the TTA site to use on my PC. I practised once every day, going over it again, again and again.'

The test gives you a scenario such as:

> Your school is organising a visit to a museum called Ardean Hall. The museum has recreated the hall as it was in the 19th century and also holds workshops for pupils. You have been asked to help with some of the arrangements, which will include a presentation to parents and a handout for pupils. The cost of the trip also needs to be calculated.
>
> Task 1 – This task involves locating the Ardean Hall Web site and adding the finishing touches to a handout for pupils. (Web browser and word processor)
> Task 2 – This task involves completing a budget and e-mail correspondence. (spreadsheet and e-mail)
> Task 3 – This task involves interrogating the database of pupils for information and adding the finishing touches to a presentation. (presentation and database)

The tasks can be completed in any order. This is the sort of thing you're asked to do for Task 1:

> You have agreed to help with the finishing touches to a handout for the visit. To do this you need to:
>
> a. locate a Web site and download a picture;
> b. add the picture and some formatting to the handout.
>
> Part 1.1 Locate the 'Ardean Hall' Web site by using the search option on the '24 Hour Museum' Web site. The 24 Hour Museum is connected to the NGfL Web site.
> Part 1.2 Locate and download the picture of 'Ardean Hall'.
> Part 1.3 Insert the picture file you have downloaded into the 'Handout' document below the heading 'View of the front of Ardean Hall'.
> Part 1.4 Insert a copyright symbol before the words 'Ardean Hall 2001'.
> (http://www.tta.gov.uk/training/skillstests/)

The standards for QTS are just the first that you'll come across in your career. The Teachers' Standards Framework (DfES, 2001) poster is very useful for getting the whole picture of what will be expected of you at different stages in your career. There are the induction standards (see Appendix 2) that have to be met after a year in the job. When you reach the top of the main pay scale you can apply to cross the Threshold, which involves meeting more standards. Then there are standards for subject leaders, SENCOs, advanced skills teachers and headteachers. I know you can't wait...

On a training course

Fitness to teach

As soon as you're offered a place on a teaching course you'll be asked to complete a form about your physical and mental health and a declaration of any criminal history. This can feel traumatic and intrusive, but is a necessary check to protect pupils.

Health

Everyone training to be a teacher has to complete a Declaration of Health form in order to prove that they are physically and mentally fit for this demanding job. This is an entry requirement for all courses that lead to qualified teacher status. Obviously, you must be completely honest: like the declaration of any criminal background, little will look worse than being dishonest. The form asks for your height, weight, and information about eyesight, hearing and whether you smoke. It has a list of major and minor ailments, such as

'Have you ever had depression?', to which you have to write a yes or a no, and then give details. It also asks, 'Are you at present taking any medicines, pills, tablets or injections?' Be precise in all answers. The doctor may ask for more information or a report from your own doctor or consultant. In a few cases, people are asked to attend a medical examination. Your declaration of health is read and assessed by the medical adviser at your training institution. He or she has to put you into one of three categories:

- A – those who are in good health or who have conditions that are not likely to interfere with efficiency in teaching;
- B – those in good health but who suffer from conditions that may interfere to some extent with efficiency in teaching;
- C – those whose condition makes them unfit to teach. Few people fit this category, and it's only used after thorough consultation.

Here is one of the questions put to the New Teacher Forum Web site:

Top tip!

Q: 'I have an interview for a PGCE (Primary) course but am concerned that my medical history may disadvantage me. I've been taking anti-depressants for the past three years. Although I no longer suffer from depression, I'm still taking the medication, albeit in very small doses, as the treatment I was prescribed must be withdrawn from gradually. Will this stop me getting on the course?'

A: No, it won't have any bearing on whether you're offered a place and it's unlikely to stop you becoming a teacher. You will have to declare your medical background, but only once you've been offered and accepted a place on a teaching course. There's no need to mention your depression at interview.

I would imagine that you would be in category A, or at worst B. Either way, it's nothing to worry about. Obviously, for your own good, you need to look after your health, and avoid anything that you know contributes to illness. Depression may creep up on you again so it's wise to make sure to let family and friends know that you want them to look out for any warning signs.

Criminal records bureau

As soon as you've been accepted for a teaching course you'll have to make a disclosure of all criminal offences, no matter how long ago. This can be uncomfortable. Take a look at the Top tip! below:

Top tip!

Q: 'I have had a six-month conditional discharge for a minor shoplifting offence from 20 years ago, when I was 18. I am ashamed and embarrassed by it. I had thought the discharge was exactly that – finished with. I've worked in primary schools for over seven years as a mum-helper, have done voluntary work with head-injured adults, counselled alcoholics and drug addicts and held a professional job in industry. Yet this summer I had to fill in a new form to do voluntary work at my children's school, and I was too embarrassed to fill it in, so have stopped helping. If I want to train as a teacher, how would it affect my employability or ability to get on a PGCE course? Do I have to declare it?'

A: The **Rehabilitation of Offenders Act 1974** was originally designed to give offenders a second chance and job prospects, so some offences become spent and no longer appear on criminal records. However, those working with children are not covered by the Act. So you should declare any offence you've committed, however long ago. A criminal record doesn't render anyone unemployable. If the conviction were for a child-related offence then it would obviously be a problem, but schools and colleges won't give too much weight to something that happened a long time ago and from which you have undoubtedly learned. What would be a far greater problem would be for you not to declare an offence. It will come to light when the Criminal Records Bureau check is made. Then the issue will not be the conviction or the 'crime', but your failure to disclose it, thereby bringing into question your basic honesty. This would clearly be much worse.

When you apply to be a teacher you'll have to apply for an enhanced disclosure from the CRB. It will show spent and unspent convictions and all cautions but will also include 'relevant non-conviction information' from police records. The CRB sends the disclosure in confidence to the prospective employer who is also obliged to treat it in strictest confidence, so don't worry about lots of people finding out about your past. For more information go to http://www.crb.gov.uk.

Study skills

People often assume that if you've got so far in the education system you won't need study skills training, but this is a mistake. You're bound to be really busy on the course and improving study skills can help to boost your efficiency.

The first thing you need to do is to get organised physically, so find a space where you can be comfortable to work. Buy yourself some files, stationery and do your best to get hold of a computer – an old word processor will be enough. Make a wall planner and draw up a timetable of when everything needs to be done by. Then work backwards from deadlines, setting yourself some smaller targets. Your college deadlines will have been well thought through by your course leader so that your considerable workload is spread over the duration of the course. If you stick to deadlines, you'll be fine. If you break them, problems will snowball and you'll end up having to write essays when you should be preparing for teaching.

Think about when you work best and what use you can make of 'dead' time – time during which you could be doing something beneficial, such as reading on the bus. Get to the library before everyone else on the course borrows the most useful books. Work with friends to share books, articles and notes. Concentrate on reading the recommended texts rather than every single item on the library shelves, and try to target the most up-to-date materials. They usually summarise the best of what has been written before. The Internet has lots of good stuff on it, but eats up time. If you're like me you'll get sidetracked. Be ruthless with your time and just go to recommended sites.

Diving into a book and working through to the end is usually unnecessary and wastes time. Be clear about what kind of information you want to find, and why. Look for relevant sections and make judicious use of the contents page, introduction and index. Scan headings and summaries. Skim read, so that you focus on the most useful parts of the work – the key points.

Making notes aids absorption and concentration and helps you summarise arguments, information and ideas. Spot and record key words or concepts. Mind maps are really useful. We quickly forget most of what we read, so put the book down and try to jot down key ideas. Don't take masses of notes or write lots of quotations.

Summarise in your own words and jot down page numbers so you can reference ideas and go back to the book if necessary.

Get into the habit of checking through your notes – writing a summary sentence can be useful. Regular review of what you have read or heard in lectures stimulates understanding so that your knowledge grows and becomes integrated with other information.

Academic referencing in essays can be tiresome if you haven't kept a list of everything you've read in the required format. So start a file of references in alphabetical order that you can cut and paste into an assignment at a later date. Check on the style that your course requires – this may not be what you're used to. Here's a standard way to reference sole-authored and multiple-authored books, and articles in academic journals, newspapers and on Web sites:

Book:
Bubb, S. (2001) *A Newly Qualified Teacher's Manual: How to Meet the Induction Standards*, David Fulton, London.

Journal article:
Bubb, S., Totterdell, M., Heilbronn, R. and Jones, C. (2002) 'How schools manage induction: "The tradition was sink or swim – now we train Olympic athletes"', *Professional Development Today*, **5** (vol no.) (3) (issue no.), autumn 2002, pp. 45–52.

Newspaper article:
Bubb, S. (2003) 'Relax. It's spring and you're loving it', *Times Educational Supplement*, Friday, 10 January 2003, pp. 22–23.

Web site:
Times Educational Supplement NQT Forum (2001) URL: www.tes.co.uk/staffroom/list_threads.asp?id=18085 (Accessed 20 October 2001).

Writing essays

For those of you who've had a break from studying, one of your greatest challenges will be actually writing an essay.

> ⌐ **From the TES forum**
>
> 'I am having a fairly nightmarish time. Finding my time management appalling and writing my first assignment well-nigh impossible. I completely lack the power to edit down and be discriminating. I have read far too many essays in edited books and have lost the power to think and articulate for myself on the heady question of the literacy strategy objectives in Y6 and 7.'

Paralysis from reading too much is very common. What you need to do is to close all books and then consider what the question wants and what *you* think. Write down the points you want to make, then think of examples from your school experience and other people's views that you've read about. Put them into some logical order so that you develop an argument. In most PGCE essays, it's important for the reader to hear your voice (use 'I'). This may be quite different to the expectations of you as an undergraduate. Don't use jargon and buzz words for their own sake. Say what you mean.

Aim small: one paragraph at a time. Just write down your ideas and don't look back until you've finished a paragraph. Yes, it probably will look awful but don't try to edit straight away. Leave it overnight and you may well be more impressed with yourself. Once you've written what you think needs to be said, you can whiz through putting in references. Don't use too many quotations, but do make sure that you can't be accused of plagiarism – your lecturers will be able to spot ideas and phrases that you've 'borrowed' without referencing.

Weave theory and practice together: 'The *Code of Practice* says … about children with special needs. I consider these aims laudable but I have found teaching an autistic boy in the mainstream classroom very difficult.'

Leave the introduction and conclusion till last. They're the most important bits and anyway, how do you know what you're going to say until you've finished it? No matter how well you plan, your work will evolve. Your introduction or abstract needs to guide the reader through your essay, so define any terms you're using, describe the context of the school experience you're drawing on and briefly outline the structure of your writing. Conclusions are very hard.

Sum up the key points you've made and perhaps try to end on a 'what needs to be done next' note.

Once you've written the essay, spend a good amount of time editing. Keep to the word limit, though going over by 10 per cent is usually acceptable. Cut out any waffle. Use British English grammar and spell-check carefully, but don't rely on that alone. It won't pick up every error that you make. Another common crime is unsubstantiated assertion – 'It is well known that...' or 'Girls learn to read more easily than boys'. Who says? Make sure that any texts you've referred to are organised alphabetically in the references section.

Once you're fairly happy with the essay, hand it in – or at least leave it alone. Avoid the temptation to hone it to perfection. Accept what is good enough – will it pass? Fine, that's all you need. Now spend your time getting ready for the next deadline.

When you get your essay back, don't just look at the grade. Read through all the comments carefully and learn from them so that you get better and better. If they don't mind, read other people's essays – particularly ones deemed to be very good so that you know what standard to aspire to.

Planning lessons

Planning lessons is a real skill and one that you'll need to develop. The QTS standards in Appendix 1 detail what is expected for planning. When you're training, it can seem like the hardest thing in the world. The different levels of planning – long, medium and short term – can cause confusion.

Long-term plans

These are the areas to teach over the course of each year, based on the National Curriculum programmes of study. Your school may well have adapted these, especially if classes are of mixed ages such as Year 3 and 4. This long-term plan is broken down into termly or half-termly chunks – the medium-term plans.

Medium-term plans

These are the units of work or main topics that pupils will be taught over a half–term or term. Usually they contain:

- the number of hours or lessons needed;
- the objectives to be covered, adjusted as appropriate for higher and lower attainers;
- opportunities to revisit topics and to make connections between different aspects;
- suggestions for activities;
- time for regular assessment and review.

Short-term plans

Short–term plans are the plans for one week or lesson. They show the nitty-gritty of how a unit of work will unfold to meet the intended objectives.

Help with planning

Long- and medium–term plans should be in place in the schools you go to, so all you have to worry about is translating them into lesson plans. There are lots of published schemes and Web sites that provide these, and that can give you some good ideas. On the standards Web site, www.standards.dfes.gov.uk/literacy (and in published folders that you'll see at college or school), there are very detailed numeracy and literacy plans. The folders have a CD ROM so you can download the plans and adapt them. There are also hundreds of plans on Curriculumonline (www.curriculumonline.gov.uk) and the Teachernet Web site (http://www.teachernet.gov.uk/TeachingandLearning/resourcematerials/Resources/). The search facility on both will help you to find over 1,000 lesson plans and resources across a wide range of subject areas and age groups. More are added all the time. The resources have been evaluated by teachers so they are good quality. However, other people's plans won't always work for your particular class and teaching style. You should be creative and confident in adapting or rejecting them to suit your needs.

Finding the right format for writing the plan is a process that you'll need to go through. Length and detail varies. Some people like to script their lessons, others just write down key points. Both are fine – if the lesson is successful. The most useful formats are easy to follow – and you need to be able to read them quickly in case there is a distraction or you lose your train of thought. Most plans have these key elements:

- date, time, subject, class;
- learning objective;
- assessment criteria;
- resources;
- teaching points and key questions;
- distribution of whole-class and group activities;
- what additional adults should do.

Start with the learning objective, chosen from the school's curriculum, then translate it into what you want the pupils to know and understand. First you need to consider what the pupils already know. This is called using assessment to inform planning – one of the standards for qualified teacher status. Good teaching involves the plan, do, assess, plan, do, assess cycle.

If you're not very focussed on a specific learning outcome, you'll run into problems. It's tempting to think of activities before considering exactly what the pupils will be learning. For instance, John wrote learning objectives such as 'characteristic features of a period', when 'learning how rich and poor children lived in Victorian times' would have been more precise. If you phrase outcomes as you would tell them to the class, you won't go far wrong. Shirley Clarke (2001) uses the acronym WALT – 'We Are Learning To'. Using such a phrase should help to keep you and the pupils focussed. Then you need to think of how to enable pupils to meet objectives, what resources to use, what activities to do and how you'll teach.

If you're new to lesson planning, it's helpful to imagine the lesson and write a chronological plan. Timings – with the resources to be used – can help pace no end. Make your introduction really tight – you can even script the main points. Start by recapping previous learning, giving the lesson objective (what they'll learn or get better at) and the 'big picture' of the lesson (what's going to happen and in what order).

Plan interesting ways for pupils to learn but check your ideas with others. I've seen some crazy things. One Year 3 teacher used a *Mr Men* book as the text to teach the literacy strategy objective: 'to discuss characters' feelings, behaviour and relationships, referring to the text'. This was not the level of text that the authors of the literacy strategy had in mind! Think about different learning styles. People learn through visual, auditory and kinaesthetic (physical interaction) stimuli. Some pupils learn better through one more than another, so aim for a mixture of them.

Differentiation is hard. You need to find out what the highest and lowest attainers can and cannot do, and then plan to allow all to make progress. Different needs can be met in a range of ways, such as:

- same task that pupils do with varying degrees of success;
- same task but with different expectations for different pupils;
- same task but with different time allocations;
- same task with an extension activity for the more able;
- adult support to enable low attainers to succeed;
- different resources to help or make the task harder;
- different tasks, but same objective;
- different objectives entirely.

Shirley Clarke's term WILF – 'What I'm Looking For' – can help you have realistic but challenging expectations. These can also be your assessment criteria. The plenary is an excellent opportunity for you and the pupils to see how the objective of the lesson has been met. Remember: the better you plan, the better the lesson will go.

Managing behaviour

Managing behaviour is one of the greatest concerns of new teachers. This book can't hope to give much help on such a complex and important topic, but there's no shortage of others devoted to the topic. Half of the battle for control lies in being organised, planning the right sort of work, and being confident. Many people who have turned out to be very good teachers started with very demanding discipline problems – so take heart, things do get better.

If you are having difficulty with control you need extra support, urgently, in establishing and maintaining the school's, and your own, behaviour policy. At a practical level, it's useful to have someone who will take miscreants off you, and someone to read the riot act for or with you. The chance remark of a friend, 'Nil carborundum' ('Don't let the ******** grind you down'), when I was having problems with a class as an experienced teacher, gave me the resolve not to give up. I changed tack, turning from a sensitive, fair teacher to a hard Hitler-like person who was not going to let the class beat her and who ruled with a rod of iron. It worked.

Getting and keeping attention are common problems. The secret is to keep lots of strategies up your sleeve. After a while, even the best ones get stale and you need to do something new. Whatever you do try to minimise your voice being used and time being wasted. Below are 20 tips from the *TES* New Teacher Forum Web site.

Top tips!

'The more negative I am and the more I shout, the more the pupils make more noise. Be calm and positive; this gives the impression that you are in control.'

'I have used a system of table points before but this is not helpful if there are some tables with mixed levels of behaviour, as it causes resentment in the ones who are trying to behave on a table where others are losing them points.'

'Display the names of all of the pupils on the board at the start of every day, or (more permanent) laminate each name onto card and affix to a board with Blutack or a felt board with Velcro. Stick a smiley face at the top of the board and agree rewards for the pupils whose name is still on the board at the end of the day/week. Clearly establish the kinds of behaviour that will result in the pupil's name staying on the board.'

'Football card system. Cut up squares of red and yellow card. In this system, like a football referee, a pupil who misbehaves is given a warning and then a yellow card. This means that if the pupil misbehaves again, he or she will get a red card, which means lost minutes at breaktime. They spend a set length of time during the next breaktime indoors, writing about exactly what they have done wrong to get the cards and what they will do in future. You then file this "signed confession" by the pupil as it can be used as evidence later if the pupil misbehaves again, for example, to be shown to parents or to headteacher. Indeed, you can even tell the pupils that if they get three red cards in a week or more they are sent to the head/get a letter sent home/other harsher punishment. This is a good system so long as you have the cards nearby. It causes no disruption to the lesson, as you don't even have to discuss it with the pupil, except briefly. You just have to make the rules consistent and clear so the pupils accept these terms as "fair and just".'

'I've found that pointing at the offenders one by one while counting them up seems to work. I've got no idea why – perhaps because they don't want to be one of the "counted" ones! When I started doing it, I asked the ones I had counted to explain why they were talking – now I just have to start counting and they stop.'

'Let them have noisy moments. I've learned to anticipate that they will have noisy moments between lessons etc, and things have become easier since I stopped expecting them to be quiet all the time.'

'Peer pressure is starting to kick in nicely in my class at the moment after having abandoned interesting lessons/discussions a few times due to disruptive kids, and giving them boring listening exercises instead. I literally stopped in mid-sentence while about to tell them where they were going for their school trip, and they had to wait until the next day to find out. Now, if they see me starting to close my book/move over to where I keep worksheets/stop mid-sentence, they quieten down.'

'If they are too noisy when coming onto the carpet for intro/plenaries I count the ones who are sitting quietly until I have counted everyone.'

'I just stop and stare at them with a "you know you are in the wrong, now do what I want" look and they shut up!'

'Simply stand at the front and raise one arm. As each pupil notices he/she raises an arm and stops talking. No one wants to be the last so they all quickly quieten down and listen.'

'Try getting a stopwatch and calmly timing how long it takes them to be quiet. Then take that time off whatever breaktime comes next! Use it in conjunction with rewards and they soon get the idea.'

'Pupils tend to be as noisy as their teacher! Basically, if you're a loud teacher, they adapt so they can hear themselves: if you're quiet, so are they. Raising your voice then immediately lowering it means they have to be much quieter to hear you.'

'Fire out the rewards (stickers etc). If you spot a couple of quiet pupils, then reward them! The rest will soon follow suit.'

'I have 30 mins written on my board at the start of the week. Every Friday they have 30 mins "golden time" where they can choose what to do. By taking off minutes of this time (or now even threatening to) works a treat.'

'Instead of having them on the carpet and bored while you're doing the register, seat them at their desks and give them a "busy book" each. Get them into the routine of coming in and doing something: handwriting, anagrams (write up a word on the board and get them to find as many other words in it as they can), number bonds, times tables, maths challenges, anything really, the more fun (and absorbing) the better! I'm a big believer in having instructions written on the board for when they come in, this way both you and they know what to expect.'

'Tell them you're going to close your eyes and when you open them they'll all be looking the right way, sitting perfectly and smiling sweetly. It's a high-risk strategy but it's never failed to work for me and at least you get to shut your eyes!'

'Turn the lights off to get everyone's attention when they're all busy.'

'Call "3, 2,1 silence".'

'Bang a drum, cymbal, etc.'

'Clap a rhythm for them to copy or "answer".'

Everyday irritating behaviour

You need to think creatively about solutions to the numerous everyday irritating behaviours, such as:

- calling out;
- fiddling;

- tapping;
- talking when you're talking;
- the whine – miiiiiiisss;
- hair-dressing;
- being out of their seats;
- farting – and the fuss from other pupils.

Just take one or two of the things that wind you up and think how you usually handle it, and then all the alternative ways you could do so. Think of your potential responses ranging from cool to very hot, slow to breaking the speed limit. You need to give yourself plenty of room for manoeuvre, so go for calm strategies at first rather than going for the jugular straight away.

Marking

You may have been warned, but nothing really prepares you for the length of time marking takes. You need a system to help you stay sane. Do the rewards, in terms of feedback to pupils that they read and act upon to improve their learning, merit the time spent on marking? I suspect you want to maximise the usefulness of marking, while allowing you time to plan, make and gather resources – and have a life. How long are you spending on marking? Try to keep a record so that you know the scale of the problem. Are you letting marking spread over a longer time than it should? It's so easy to do.

If you want to cut down time spent on marking you need to look at whether you're making the most of all the different sorts of marking. Estimate how much marking (of class work and homework) you have to do in a week and at what level. Remember that peer review and self-assessment are very valuable as well as potentially less time-consuming for you since you'll be in the role of 'moderator'. Balance out work that needs marking over the week so that you don't have too much at one go. Decide what seems a realistic amount of time to spend on marking and when you could get it done to fit in with other commitments. Try to stick to your 'timetable', aiming to reduce the time and to do things earlier and more quickly, if possible.

Different sorts of marking

There are many different sorts of marking. Perhaps you could benefit from extending your range:

- children 'marking' their own and each other's work;
- self-assessment;
- pupils marking their work during the plenary;
- quick ticking and checking as pupils work;
- using stampers ('Good effort', 'Excellent!');
- using codes (sp, underline) that pupils understand rather than full sentences;
- grading;
- selective marking – ignoring all but answers to key questions;
- brief comment against the learning intention;
- detailed comment against the learning intention;
- traffic light marking – pupils putting a green mark against work where they feel they've met the learning objective or a red mark where they haven't understood it, enabling teachers to prioritise those pupils with difficulties.

You'll probably find that different pieces of work require different levels of marking. There will be occasions when a Rolls Royce product is needed but at other times something more everyday is fine. Once you get to know the expectations of the school and the pupils' work rate you can design a marking schedule to help you manage what can be a very stressful burden. Ask your colleagues how they manage their marking. How long does it take them? When do they do it? What tips do they have for you? Little things such as collecting books so that they're open at the right page for marking can make a real difference.

Ask to see some examples of other people's marking to get a feel for what is really expected, but avoid the temptation to do a more rigorous job – a one-upmanship that will generally make your induction year even harder. Stern (1999) suggests building a bank of useful marking phrases and questions, instead of the everyday 'Good', to help you.

Do you deliberately plan work that doesn't take so long to mark, but which still meets learning objectives? If you're clear about the learning intention for the lesson, you should be able to write some specific assessment criteria – the things that pupils might do towards meeting the learning intention partially or fully. Shirley Clarke (2001) recommends using the acronyms WALT and WILF. WALT (We Are Learning To) is a way of sharing the learning intention with pupils. This can then be refined for different groups of pupils through telling them WILF (What I'm Looking For). If you are using worksheets, consider writing assessment criteria directly onto them for you to make some abbreviated judgements against. These can be differentiated for different groups of pupils.

Peer review is a very useful form of marking. Plan some time for pupils to swap books and 'mark' each other's. Ideally do this before the end of the lesson so that they can improve their work before the lesson finishes. This will be truly formative marking. Pupils are rarely silly or rude about each other's work, but you'll need to consider your pairings carefully and come down hard on those who do not approach their responsibilities sensibly. Putting people who are friends and whose work is of a similar standard together works well. If you have an assistant, deploy them to help those who have difficulty reading and writing. Pairing people who speak the same mother tongue can also be advantageous, because they can explain things to each other in their own language.

Obviously, pupils will copy the marking style that they have experienced so your one-to-one marking will have countless spin-offs. The above procedure will also be useful for you to use. Follow the school or department marking policy and decide on your own additional one. Note points that many pupils had difficulty with, on a lesson plan so that it can feed into teaching. Try to focus on marking against assessment criteria – how well they have met the learning objectives. This is easier said than done, particularly in a piece full of errors. What are you going to do about spelling mistakes, for instance? What about handwriting, grammar and punctuation? When will the pupils have time to read and respond to your marking, by correcting and learning spellings for example?

Learning from observing others

Whatever stage you're at in the profession, you'll learn a great deal about teaching from watching others doing it. Similarly the more you watch children learning, and think about the problems that they have, the better your teaching will be. Trainee teachers do a great deal of observing colleagues and newly qualified teachers find it the most useful of all induction activities (Totterdell *et al*, 2002).

Make the most of your training opportunities to observe other teachers. Try to watch a range of teachers and assistants, age groups, subjects and lessons at different times of the day. It's very cheering to see that everyone has similar problems and fascinating to study the different ways people manage them. Don't always observe experienced and successful teachers. You'll learn a great deal from seeing other trainees, NQTs, assistants and supply teachers. If you watch a class you've taught being led by someone else you can see the pupils' learning, behaviour and reactions, and how another teacher handles them.

However, observing so that you get something out of it is not easy. You need to have a focus for your observation. There is so much to see that you can end up getting overwhelmed. First, decide what you want to observe. Ideally, link the observation to something that you have problems with or want to develop.

Once you have decided what you'd like to observe, you need to arrange it. You need to discuss what you want to observe with the teacher. Remember that they're doing you a favour and may be apprehensive about you being in the classroom so you'll need to be sensitive. Tell them what you'd like to see and why. Ask if you can look at planning related to the lesson. It's essential to look at teaching in relation to learning. Always think about cause and effect. Why are the pupils behaving as they are? The cause is usually related to teaching.

Make sure you sit where you can see both the teacher and the pupils, and look at what high, average and low attainers accomplish. Jot down things of interest. You may want to note certain phrases that teachers use to get attention, ways they organise tidying-up time, etc. You can use a blank piece of paper for this, but a form with prompts helps keep you focussed (see Figures 3.1, 3.2). Afterwards, reflect on the teaching and learning you've seen – ideally in discussion with the person you observed. Perhaps it inspired a brainwave, unrelated to what you saw. Write a few bullet points about what you've learned, and the ideas that could be implemented.

Teacher: Subject: Learning objective:		Date and time: Additional adults:
Prompts:	OK	Comments. What has the teacher done to get this response?
Pay attention		
Behave well		
Relate well to adults and pupils		
Are interested		
Understand what to do		
Understand why they're doing an activity		
Gain new knowledge, skills		
Speak and listen well		
Have errors corrected		
Work hard		
Act responsibly		
Understand how well they have done		
Understand how they can improve		
Enjoy the lesson		

Figure 3.1 Lesson observation sheet – how well pupils learn (Bubb, 2001: 90)

Being observed

You'll probably be observed about once a week when you're training. It's almost always a stressful experience, but try to see it as an opportunity to get some really useful feedback and as a way to develop – not as a threat. The value of observation, however, depends on how well it is planned, executed and discussed afterwards.

The people observing you may also find it stressful. Much teacher training is done in partnership with schools, so you may have people observing you who feel inexperienced and uncertain of the best way

Observer:		Observation started ...... ended ......
Teacher and year group:		
Subject and learning objective:		
Prompts:	OK	Comments and evidence. What impact does teaching have on pupils?
Planning		
Ground rules		
Behaviour management		
Expectations		
Organisation		
Resources		
Shares learning objectives		
Subject knowledge		
Explanations		
Teaching strategies		
Voice		
Pace		
Use of time		
Questioning		
Motivating		
Differentiation		
Additional adults		
Feedback		
Activities		
		Time: Pupils on task:...... off task:......
Plenary		Time: Pupils on task:...... off task:......

Figure 3.2   Lesson observation sheet – prompts for looking at teaching (Bubb, 2001: 91)

to go about it. They will also be mindful of the responsibility to help you make progress, while maintaining a good relationship. This can lead some to be too kind. Trainees sometimes feel that they are not being sufficiently challenged. This is particularly true if you're very successful, but you too need to be helped to develop professionally.

You can help this process by being very open to ideas and accepting and even encouraging constructive criticism. Phrases such as 'That's a really good idea. Thanks' will work wonders.

Before an observation

To get the most from an observation, think about what you'd like the observer to look out for: a problem you're having. Far from being an admission of failure, this will show that you're a reflective practitioner who wants to improve. You'll feel better about the observation if you're completely prepared. If you know when you'll be seen, plan with even more care and have a copy of the lesson plan for the observer. Be absolutely clear about what you want the pupils to learn and achieve by the end of the lesson, and make sure that your teaching and the activities enable them to do so. Really think through every stage of the lesson to pre-empt problems – transitions from one thing to another are usually tricky. Have as much as possible written on the board beforehand.

Think about what the person observing you is looking for. Address things that haven't gone well before. Look at the QTS standards again. Obviously, you'll want to show that you're making progress against your current objectives too. Look at the form that the observation will be written on, such as the one in Figure 3.3. All observers have their own pet loves and hates that will affect how they look at your teaching, so plan to please!

Most importantly, look after yourself so that you're on top form for the lesson that will be observed. Try to get a good night's sleep the night before so that you're not too tired. Eat and drink things that make you feel good. Avoid too much caffeine. Do everything you can to feel confident – wear your favourite teaching clothes, encourage other people to boost you up. Tell yourself that you're going to teach well, and believe it.

Coping with nerves

Being nervous when observed is perfectly normal, and most people can tell when you are and make allowances for this. One way of coping with nerves is to understand why you get worried: then you can do something about it. Common concerns and possible solutions are listed in Figure 3.4.

Date:	Time:	Year:	Grouping:
Observation no:		Subject:	Context:

3.1 Planning, expectations and targets

3.1.1 3.1.2 3.1.3 3.1.4 3.1.5 3.1.6

3.2 Monitoring and assessment

3.2.1 3.2.2 3.2.3 3.2.4 3.2.5 3.2.6 3.2.7

3.3 Teaching and class management

3.3.1 3.3.2 a b c d 3.3.3 3.3.4 3.3.5 3.3.6 3.3.7 3.3.8 3.3.9 3.3.10
3.3.11 3.3.12 3.3.13 3.3.14

Overall comment:

Figure 3.3 Classroom observation format – the QTS standards (Bubb and Mulholland, 2003)

During the observation

Give the observer a copy of your plan so that they are clear why you are doing certain things, but otherwise just block out the observer and focus on teaching and learning. Think of your teaching as a performance, and go for gold. Try to keep to time, but be flexible where necessary. Don't forget to have a plenary to reinforce and assess learning. Try to demonstrate the standards. Be particularly organised with resources. Don't feel inhibited by the presence of the observer – try to be natural.

Your concern	Possible solutions
Pupils will be passive – won't engage, answer questions, etc	Plan something to get them lively. Use talk partners ('turn to your neighbour and tell them the answer to my question').
The behaviour of a certain child will ruin everything	Ask someone else to have the child for that lesson; plan for an assistant to be with the child; warn the observer.
I can't get or keep the class's attention	Do your best; plan well with this in mind; try suggested strategies; have as much written on the board beforehand as possible; but maybe look on the observation as a way to get really specific advice; warn the observer.
The pupils play up when I'm observed	Tell them that they are being observed. Remind them that you are expecting exemplary behaviour.
Technology will go wrong	Set it up beforehand; check and double-check; have a back up if it does go wrong.
I'll forget or lose key resources	Make a list of what you need, tick items off when collected, organise them.
The teaching assistant won't turn up	Keep reminding them that you're relying on them and give them a plan of what they should do.
The pupils will finish work too early	Have some extension work; make the task harder or open-ended.
I'll forget what I planned to do	Do a clear written plan – that very act helps lodge it in your mind; keep your plan to hand on a distinctive clipboard to avoid it getting lost; have a spare just in case you leave it somewhere; use prompt cards; rehearse the lesson structure in your mind.
I'll forget what to say	Script key parts of the lesson, especially questions; rehearse out loud and in your head.
I'll let the class wander off the point of the lesson	Stay focussed; put timings on your plan and try to stick to them; write up the learning objective; plan questions that will guide the pupils' thinking.

Figure 3.4   Common concerns about observations

Don't panic if things start to go wrong. Think on your feet. Most trainees have some lessons that go swimmingly, others that are okay and some that are a disaster. There are a huge number of factors to do with you and what you're teaching and then a whole heap to do with different classes, what lesson they've just had, what the weather's like and what time of day it is.

The post-observation discussion

After the lesson, think about what the pupils learned and why, so that you're ready to answer the inevitable 'How do you think it went?' question. What were you pleased with? What could have gone better? How did your teaching affect the progress pupils made? Don't be disheartened if the lesson didn't go well. See it as an event to be learnt from and given advice on. It was a one-off performance, a snapshot, and things can be different tomorrow.

Use the feedback to discuss the minutiae of the lesson, and to get ideas for improvements. There's no such thing as a perfect teacher (except in your mind) so your lesson doesn't have to be perfect. You need to show that you're reflective, making progress and acting on advice. Most of all show that you want advice – don't be defensive. Be aware of your body language and notice that of the person giving you feedback. You want to come across as earnest and reflective. A large proportion of communication is non-verbal, so:

- lean slightly forward;
- uncross your arms;
- make eye contact;
- smile and nod;
- listen actively.

Listen well: don't just hear what you want or expect to hear. Focus on what is being said rather than how it is being said and see it as information rather than criticism. Make notes of salient points. Paraphrase and summarise what the observer says. This helps you concentrate on what is being said and is very helpful in getting a clear understanding of their view. It involves reflecting back your interpretation of what you have heard, which can be very useful for the observer. Use phrases such as 'So what you mean is...', 'In other words...'.

However, if you think your teaching is criticised unfairly make sure you explain the reasoning behind your actions. Stick up for yourself, though in an utterly professional way. Ask for clarification of anything you're unsure of, examples and suggestions of how you could have done things differently. Try to get lots of advice and ideas that you can go away with and mull over. Afterwards, reflect on the discussion. Feel good about the positive comments (there will always be some) and think about how to improve.

four

Looking after yourself

- Being aware of the stages you might go through
- Looking after yourself
- Looking after your voice
- Managing your time

Your training and the first year in teaching will be rewarding and stimulating, but they will undoubtedly be hard and very stressful. In this chapter, I will look at ways to make it easier on a very practical level.

Being aware of the stages you might go through

There is a common perception that a teacher should be able to teach well. Certainly, the pupils taught by a trainee or newly qualified teacher have as much right to a good education as those taught by someone with 20 years' experience. However, there is a huge difference between novice and experienced teachers. Like any skill or craft, learning to teach is a developmental process characterised by devastating disasters and spectacular successes. Teaching is a job that can never be done perfectly – one can always improve. The more I know about teaching and learning the more I realise there is to know. This is what makes it such a great job – but also such a potentially depressing one.

How you feel about teaching will probably change on a daily basis at first. One day will be great and leave you feeling positive and idealistic, but the next will be diabolical. As time goes on, good days outnumber the bad ones, and you will realise that you are actually enjoying the job. There are recognised stages that teachers go through. Appreciating them will help to keep you going and help you realise that you will need different levels and types of support at different times during your training and induction years. I have used Furlong and Maynard's (1995) five stages of development that teachers go through to illustrate the development that might happen to you (see Figure 4.1).

Stage	Characteristics
Early idealism	Feeling that everything is possible and having a strong picture of how you want to teach ('I'll never shout'). This is a fantasy stage where you imagine pupils hanging on your every word.
Survival	Reality strikes. You live from day to day, needing quick fixes and tips. You find it hard to solve problems because there are so many of them. Behaviour management is of particular concern – you have nightmares about losing control. You are too stressed and busy to reflect. Colds and sore throats seem permanent. Survival often characterises the middle of teaching practice and the second half of the first term for NQTs.
Recognising difficulties	You can see problems more clearly. You can identify difficulties and think of solutions because there is some space in your life. You move forward. A skilled mentor or induction tutor aids this stage considerably.
Hitting the plateau	Key problems, such as behaviour management and organisation, have been solved so you feel things are going well. You feel you are mastering teaching. You begin to enjoy it and don't find it too hard, but you don't want to tackle anything different or take on any radical new initiatives. If forced you will pay lip service to new developments. Some teachers spend the rest of their career at this stage.
Moving on	You are ready for further challenges. You want to try out different styles of teaching, new age groups, take more responsibilities.
Activity 1. What stage do you think you are in at the moment? 2. Where do you want to be and by when? 3. What can you do to move on? 4. Who can help you?	

Figure 4.1 Five stages that teachers go through

Looking after yourself

If your experiences are like mine, illness will plague you during your training and first year of teaching like it has never done before. By illness I am not talking about anything serious – just the low-level depressing rounds of sore throats, coughs and colds. Large numbers of children mean a lot of germs! When you're busy the easiest thing to do is to forget to look after yourself. Everyone knows that they function better with good nutrition and rest, but these seem to be the first things to be neglected. Also notice the signs of stress – problems with sleep, eczema, etc. They are signals to you from your body that should not be ignored for long. The following are some common sense tips for looking after yourself:

- Try to organise accommodation so that your journey is reasonable and that you feel comfortable when you get home.
- Remember to eat – don't skip meals. Snack on nutritious, high-energy foods such as bananas rather than chocolate bars. Get organised at weekends so that you have enough suitable food to last the week.
- Take vitamin supplements. Vitamins and minerals are essential in helping your body fight off all the viruses that the pupils will bring into school. Some people swear by Echinacea.
- Watch out for head lice – check your hair frequently with a very fine nit comb and take immediate action if you find any.
- Watch your caffeine and biscuit intake – the staple diet of many staffrooms! They really aren't much good for you.
- Take exercise and get some fresh air during the school day. It's a good idea to leave the building at lunchtime to get these. You'll feel better for a short break.
- Doing some serious exercise once a week will be of great benefit – join a class, play tennis or whatever. Teaching makes you feel very tired but exercise will give you more energy. You function better all round if you are fit.
- Plan into your life some 'me' time. Do whatever makes you feel better. This might be soaking in a hot bath, reading novels or watching escapist films. Also, keep a social life. This is likely to be limited, but is essential.
- Avoid stress, as far as possible. This is not easy in teaching, but there are certain people and situations that increase one's blood pressure, so avoid them as far as possible.
- Don't over-commit yourself. Don't offer to do things to earn favour. If someone asks you to do something, remember that you can always say no.

- See teaching as acting. Each lesson is a performance and if one goes badly the next can go better. Separate the performance from the real you. This will stop you feeling too wretched about lessons that don't go well. Remember that few people are natural born teachers – everyone has to work at it and everyone can get better.
- Pace yourself. You can't afford to burn out. Plan some days to be less demanding. Recognise the peaks and troughs in your daily energy levels and organise yourself accordingly.
- Set yourself time limits and work limits, and stick to them.

Looking after your voice

Perhaps one of the most important tools teachers have is their voice – without it we are lost. Teachers use their voices as much as the busiest professional actor, but do so day in day out and without training. Tension restricts your voice and can cause lasting damage. In training and your first year of teaching, if not throughout your career, you are likely to suffer problems with your voice. It is worth trying to look after it. Here are some examples of things that are bad for your voice:

- Excessive or forceful coughing or throat clearing. These put a great strain on your voice and are often habits rather than physical necessities.
- Drinking tea, coffee, fizzy drinks or alcohol. These dehydrate the body.
- Constantly placing demands on the voice, such as shouting or speaking above the pupils.
- Speaking or singing when the voice is tired or sore.
- Whispering. This is just as harmful as shouting because it strains the voice.
- Speaking in a forceful or tense manner.
- Being tense. The voice is part of the muscle and breathing system, both of which suffer when you are stressed, so the ability to relax is essential.
- Smoke, chalk dust, felt-tip pen fumes, chlorine, etc, are all bad for your voice.

- Continuing to speak with a sore throat, using maskers such as painkillers, throat sweets or sprays that provide temporary relief.

Ideas for looking after your voice

Think of all the strategies you can use to engage your pupils that don't involve your voice. Consider body language, signals and gesture, where you position yourself, encouraging and developing pupils' listening skills, and agreed signals (whistle, song, time out gesture). Find non-verbal ways to get attention. You might use a drum, cymbal, or triangle, clap a rhythm that the pupils have to repeat back to you, or raise a hand. The look, the smile, the glare, the raised eyebrow, the tut can be more effective than words – and so can a theatrical silence or closing of a book. Listen to yourself teaching (use a tape recorder) – are you using enough intonation to keep attention, unnecessarily repeating things, talking over the pupils, or talking too much? Other tips include:

- Drink more water. Aim for six to eight glasses of still water each day.
- For more volume without shouting, project your voice. Open your mouth more and try to speak from the lungs rather than the throat.
- Inhale steam to relax a tired or sore throat.
- Breathe in a relaxed, focussed manner, avoiding lifting shoulders and upper chest.
- Find someone to massage your neck and shoulders to relax this area.
- Allow your voice periods of rest.
- In the classroom, use your voice with care and economy. Aim to say things only once – some teachers get into the habit of repeating almost everything they say!
- When whole-class teaching, emphasise key words orally, and write them on the board for added effect.
- Where possible move to your listeners, rather than calling out. Position yourself so that everyone can see your lips and hear you at your most comfortable volume.
- Plan for learning to occur through pupil-talk rather than always through teacher-talk.

- If you need to shout, shout the first word then quieten down. For instance, 'STOP what you're doing and look this way.' Lower the pitch to sound more authoritative and avoid squeaking.
- Don't try to talk over pupils. If you talk while they are chatting they might stop talking, but the chances are they'll just carry on at a louder level.
- Don't cough to clear your throat too often – swallow or yawn instead.

Look out for damage to your voice, for which you should seek medical advice:

- a hoarse voice that persists;
- change in vocal quality, pitch, sudden shifts in pitch, breaks in the voice;
- vocal fatigue for no apparent reason;
- tremors in the voice;
- pain while speaking;
- loss of voice.

Managing your time

If you're to survive, let alone make the most of your training years, you need to get into the habit of using your time well. Perhaps you're already ruthlessly efficient in this area, one of those people for whom even trash TV watching seems to be purposeful. Most people, however, feel that they have too much to do in too little time. It's one of the main reasons people give for leaving the profession. It's such a problem that the DfES (2003a) is spending a great deal of time and money on restructuring the teaching workforce so that everyone can work fewer hours, and spend time on the most useful aspects of the job. Get into good habits while you're training.

Knowing how you're spending time

Whether you're at college, or in a school, it's useful to see how you spend your time. Complete the chart in Figure 4.2 for one week to get a feel for whether you have a work–life balance. 'Me time' should include anything that you feel better for, such as socialising, going out, exercise, watching a favourite TV programme, reading, soaking in the bath, talking to someone you like. Under 'domestic' put basic every day living – cooking, shopping, tidying, washing, cleaning, talking to people at home, eating.

You don't have to be precise in allocating time, but does each day

	Working at school/college	Working at home	Travel	Domestic	Me time	Sleep
Sunday						
Monday						
Tuesday						
Wednesday						
Thursday						
Friday						
Saturday						
Total						

Figure 4.2 How do you spend your time?

add up roughly to 24 hours? If it's under, maybe you, like me, find that time just disappears. This is lovely if you're on holiday – in fact it's one of the marks of a relaxed day when I can't think what I've done with my time… and I don't care. When you're becoming a teacher though, disappearing hours can be dangerous because there's just too much to do and you'll get behind.

Look at your chart. What are you doing too little of? If you don't get enough sleep, noisy classrooms are unbearable so that's a definite one to keep an eye on. Is there any way that travel time can be reduced by, say, going to work or college before the morning rush hour and leaving before the evening one starts? If you use public transport could you get anything done in travel time – marking, planning, thinking, some 'me time' reading, or a quick nap? A journey can be a good way to wind down after a day's work. I know a teacher who returned to her old job that had a long journey because the new one had a journey so short that there seemed to be no gap between work and home, so no winding down time. For those of you with dependants at home, travelling may be the only time you get to yourself.

Using time well

It's useful to think about the quality of your time as well as the quantity available. It's worth recognising which part of the day – or night – is the most productive for you – the time when you have your most creative ideas, or can concentrate best. For the majority of people this is early in the day, when they are freshest. A minority of people do their best work late at night.

About 20 per cent of our time is prime time and, used well, it should produce about 80 per cent of our most creative and productive work. The rest of your time is likely to be of lower quality, and is nowhere near as productive. In this low quality time, plan to do things that are easy to pick up after interruptions or jobs that you look forward to doing.

Lesson planning, writing essays and other difficult jobs need high quality time. If you try to do them at times when you'll be interrupted or are tired and hungry you'll become frustrated, and everything will take longer. You also need to consider where you work best: take a look at this question posted to the New Teacher Forum in Top tip!

Top tip!

Q: 'I just get so annoyed that being in the building seems to equate in so many people's minds with being committed. It seems to me that most of it is mere presentism. Am I alone in finding that I work far more efficiently at home, where I am not surrounded by others and can focus much more efficiently on lesson preparation, marking or admin?'

A: It seems to be the done thing in primary schools at least to stay as long as possible – there's definitely a competitive element to it. I've known teachers who came in at 7.00 or 7.30 am and stayed until 5.30 pm or later, and still went home with huge amounts of work. Let's face it, if you're a teacher who cares even a little bit about the quality of work you do you will be investing massive amounts of your own time on the job outside of directed hours. Indeed, you could work all the time if you were so inclined and still have more things to do: evenings, weekends, holidays. There's always room for work, but you need a life too.

Work smarter not harder

The DfES is committed to reducing teacher workload. Areas in which you could reduce worktime are: admin, planning, marking, making resources and worksheets, and display. Here are some ideas to help you do so:

- Prioritise.
- Compartmentalise – set boundaries, especially when working at home.
- Accept 'good enough'.
- Avoid stressful people and time bandits.
- Set yourself targets – don't add to them.
- When do you work best? Fit work around energy highs and lows.
- What work can be done in lows?
- Set boundaries to tasks – time, quality, quantity.
- Build in rewards.
- Draw up an action plan of how you'll reduce time on specific tasks. Remember that a tired teacher is rarely an effective teacher.

part two

Your first year

Looking for a job

There's a great deal to consider when thinking about working as a teacher. You'll want to know that you'll be supported in your first year so you need to be clear about the induction systems, particularly because they vary between different parts of the United Kingdom. There are so many different sorts of schools. You need to factor into the equation financial incentives; whether to opt for the independent or state sector; supply teaching; working abroad; moving between primary, secondary and special; and what sort of school will suit you. Are you clear what you want?

Which country

Even before you think about which school, you should decide which country to work in. Most people teach in the country they trained in, but moving even within the United Kingdom can be difficult because the regulations and induction systems vary. However, each country within the European Economic Area recognises each other's induction qualifications so you won't have to repeat your first year if you move.

The entry qualifications to be a teacher differ between England, Northern Ireland, Wales and Scotland. For instance, Northern Ireland, England and Wales require teachers to have GCSE maths and English at C grade, a relevant degree and qualified teacher status. Scotland requires primary teachers to have maths at Standard Grade 2, which is equivalent to a GCSE B grade. All teachers must have Higher grade English at band C, which is equivalent to having both English language and literature GCSE at C grade. These variations could be a barrier if a primary teacher with maths GCSE only at C grade and a D in English literature planned to move to Scotland. The General Teaching Council of Scotland is rigorous about qualifications and you must register in order to teach. The PGCE and BEd are recognised by the Scottish GTC but not the GTP and RTP.

You may want to work further afield, outside Europe. No matter how good the support is for new teachers or how 'British' the school, it won't count as induction for UK purposes so you'll have to do induction in the United Kingdom when you return. Take a look at the Top tip! below, answering a query about this to the New Teacher Forum.

Top tip!

Q: 'I'm doing a PGCE but plan to go abroad, probably to teach English in Japan. Will this be detrimental to my chances of getting employment when I return? Is there a set period of time within which I must do my NQT year, before the PGCE qualification becomes redundant?'

A: There isn't any time limit between getting your teaching qualification and starting your induction year in England, though lots of people think there is. The Golden Hello and Repayment of Teacher Loans are the only things that have time limits to them. Your PGCE never runs out and can't get taken away from you. You've got it for life – and the qualified teacher status that goes with it. However, you can fail induction, which means you aren't allowed to teach in a state school or non-maintained special school in England ever again. So it makes sense to do induction in your first year of teaching when all that you've learnt is fresh and up to date, and in the context that you trained for. Going abroad is going to make a complex job harder, and you may not get the reduced timetable, support, monitoring and assessment that will help you be a better teacher.

Having taught abroad won't be detrimental to getting employment in England – but I don't suppose it'll help if you're competing with people fresh from training and up to date with the latest educational developments. Employers may feel that your professionalism has been enriched through teaching abroad or they may question your commitment to the job and staying at their school. There will always be schools with vacancies, but these are often ones in 'challenging circumstances' with a high staff turnover – not brilliant places to do induction.

You also need to question whether you should teach abroad when your own country has invested in training you and needs you desperately. Working abroad may seem glamorous, especially when you're interviewed in a swanky London hotel, but many postings on the Teaching Overseas part of the *TES* Web site tell a very different story, so do research the school carefully before signing any contract.

Here are some real life experiences of some of the visitors to the *TES* Web site:

From the *TES* forum

'Every time my employers decide to make cutbacks they change our contracts, altering bonuses, etc. Unfortunately we have to accept or leave.'

'They do not put money into staff training.'

'Normally what you are told in interviews is often what you want to hear. They talk of palm trees, the Red Sea, amazing pupil teacher ratios and the tax-free salary. It feels different when you get into the classroom and face 27 very mixed ability, mixed English, indifferent, rude, obnoxious pupils.'

'English is not widely spoken so you may feel isolated if you come by yourself.'

continued overleaf

> ### continued
>
> 'Resources were few, communication was poor, there appeared to be no genuine educational vision and the school did not enforce its own rules and published standards.'
>
> 'They are into making money, and you are going to help them make money!'
>
> 'Despite the glossy brochures and many promises, when I arrived there was a 100 per cent new staff!'
>
> 'Many schools do not appear to have a salary structure they are willing to make public.'
>
> 'Living abroad is a culture shock.'

International schools range from the appalling to the outstanding. Before accepting a teaching position, speak to or e-mail someone who works at the school and ask specific questions about salary, accommodation, classroom resources, the sorts of pupils and teaching workload.

Financial incentives

England and Wales have financial incentives for teachers of shortage subjects that you'll want to bear in mind when deciding what sort of school you want to work in.

Golden Hellos

You can claim the £4,000 Golden Hello in England and Wales if you're taking a PGCE in secondary maths, science, English, modern foreign languages, Welsh, design and technology or information & communications technology (http://www.dfes.gov.uk/go4itnow/golden-hellos.shtml). However, it's not really a Golden 'Hello' so much as a way to get you working for longer because you can only claim the money in the term after you've successfully completed induction and if you're still teaching that shortage subject in a maintained school. Unfortunately, this doesn't include colleges and other places that don't have standard school status. Here are some interesting cases, posted to the Forum, none of whom were eligible for the Golden Hello:

From the **TES forum**

'I did a PGCE last year and currently teach IT at Greenwich College, so am I eligible for a Golden Hello?' Diana

'We are science teachers. Our school was state maintained, but it was closed in August and reopened in September as a City Academy. We've been told that as we are not now a maintained school we can't have our Golden Hello.' John and Lucy

Diana definitely isn't entitled to a Golden Hello since she works in the Further Education sector. John and Lucy's school is technically right in saying it doesn't have to give Golden Hellos as it's a City Academy. Only teachers in maintained or non-maintained special schools are eligible for the £4,000. Morally, however, I think the two teachers in this example should be given the money since they joined the school thinking that it was one! If they left and went to a state school, they'd get it – so that could be a threat they might want to use. If I were a headteacher I wouldn't want to lose them or make science teachers feel disgruntled in any way. If you find yourself in a similar position, before you actually start looking for other jobs, think about how happy you are in your school, what promotion prospects it offers and whether moving to another school will be worth £4,000 – on which you will of course be taxed.

In order to actually claim the Golden Hello you have to fill in the form that you were probably given when you were training, and send it to your LEA. If you've lost it, you can get another from your LEA or the DfES.

You don't need to have been in continuous employment for the Golden Hello. In fact, you can have about three and half years out since the rule is that you can have the Golden Hello as long as, within five years of qualifying as a teacher, you have finished induction (one year minimum) and are working in a state school. You just need proof that you've passed induction. You have to be teaching the shortage subject that you qualified in, so the person in the Inbox below would not be eligible.

From the **TES forum**

'My PGCE was in Business Studies but I've now finished induction and am teaching maths in a state school. Am I eligible for the Golden Hello?'

The Repayment of Teacher Loans (RTL) scheme

The RTL, the Repayment of Teacher Loans scheme (Student Loans Company, 2002), is a fantastic deal – all the loans taken out while you were a student are paid off! A not untypical NQT borrowed £6,500 during her first degree and £4,800 in her PGCE year. So her £11,300 debt and the interest accrued will be paid off. Wow!

Unfortunately there's lots of small print. For a start, the only people eligible for this fabulous deal are those who qualified after 1 February 2002. However, it applies to all routes into teaching – not just the PGCE. It's open to people working in maintained schools, non-maintained special schools but, unlike the Golden Hello, also City Technology Colleges, City Colleges for the Technology of the Arts and City Academies in England and Wales. You have to have a permanent or fixed term contract of at least eight continuous weeks with the school or Local Education Authority – not a supply agency. There are also deals for people in Further Education colleges. In this respect the RTL is much fairer than the Golden Hello, which is limited to those with PGCEs and excludes people in CTCs, City Academies and FE.

However, it is only for people who teach maths, science, modern foreign languages, English (including drama), Welsh, design & technology, or ICT for at least half of their teaching time in a normal week. I bet those of you who teach geography, history, RE, PE, music or art feel really sick. First, no Golden Hello; now, no loans repaid. Pretty demotivating stuff, especially if you work harder than those getting the goodies. It's not fair but I guess the DfES isn't trying to be. Its aim is to recruit for shortage subjects and tempt people with certain degrees into teaching rather than industry or finance.

Primary teachers have been told that they are eligible if they teach shortage subjects to classes other than their own and do so for half the week. This is blatantly discriminatory since primary schools aren't organised like that. So, in practice, the RTL won't be an option for many in the primary sector, though one or two people who teach sets as well as their class have been successful.

It's really important to know that to be eligible for the RTL you have to start teaching within *seven* months of gaining QTS. For most people that will mean February, but the date on your QTS certificate from the DfES is crucial in determining the seven months exactly. This time limit will come as a blow to those people who want to travel or teach abroad.

However, for those NQTs in areas without a teacher shortage the seven-month limit is a significant headache, especially when they already have to contend with England's induction Four Term Rule – you can't do short-term supply once four terms has elapsed from the first day's work unless you've completed induction.

Lastly, you need to have an outstanding loan debt with the Student Loans Company (SLC). The scheme does not repay money borrowed from family, friends or banks. Nor does it have any reward for those people who got jobs while studying, scrimped and got by without taking out big loans with the SLC. I'm worried that it'll cause people to run up large debts with the expectation that they'll be repaid – and what if they're not? The rules change all the time. Please note that the RTL is called a *pilot* scheme. At the moment, it's only due to run for people who start teaching in 2002/03, 2003/04 and 2004/05.

The scheme will repay whatever amount is outstanding when you start work as a teacher in an eligible post. Don't make any voluntary payments, or let generous relatives do so as a graduation present, or you'll lose out.

Now we come to the biggie. The debts aren't paid off in one go. Your student loans will be paid off over 10 years for full-time teachers with income contingent loans, or around five to seven years for those with older mortgage-style loans. So, although you can move schools, you can't stop being a teacher of those shortage subjects in the state sector. If you do, you'll have to start making the loan repayments yourself.

If you think you're eligible, you have to get an application form from the Student Loans Company (0870 240 6298). If you want to check whether you're eligible ring the Teaching Information Line on 0845 6000991 or 6000992 for Welsh speakers.

Are you eligible to have your loans repaid?

If you

1. work in a maintained school, a non-maintained special school, a City Technology College, a City College for the Technology of the Arts or a City Academy in England or Wales;
2. teach maths, science, MFL, English (including drama), Welsh, DT, or ICT for at least half of your timetable, and started teaching within seven months of gaining QTS;
3. have a contract of at least eight continuous weeks with a school or LEA;
4. have QTS that was awarded after 1 February 2002;
5. have an outstanding loan debt with the Student Loans Company

then apply to have your loans repaid!

Types of school

Maintained sector

Most schools are in the maintained sector, which means that they are funded and controlled by the state. However, there are lots of different schools around. Most are maintained by the DfES and LEAs and are known as 'community schools', though ones with Foundation school status have more independence from the LEA. The governing body, rather than the LEA, is the employer and the admissions authority. Some schools have awards or specialist status. Others are based around a certain faith. Adverts usually refer to what status or awards the school has. The most common awards are:

- Artsmark for excellence in the arts – different levels, the top of which is gold;
- Sportsmark for excellence in sport;

- Investors in People – an award for organisations that look after their staff well;
- School Achievement Award – awarded by the DfES for schools that have vastly improved their SATs results.

There is a confusing array of types of schools – and one school can carry several labels and hold several awards. There are Advanced, Specialist, Beacon, Training and Faith schools, as well as all sorts of Academies.

Advanced schools

Advanced schools are successful, progressive secondary schools that perform consistently well in relation to their circumstances, are recognised for their particular areas of expertise, already work closely and effectively in collaboration with other secondary schools and have the energy and capacity to lead transformation across the education system.

Specialist schools

Specialist schools have been designated by the government to have a special focus on their chosen subject area. They must meet the full national curriculum requirements and deliver a broad and balanced education to all pupils, as well as specialising in their chosen subject area, which could be one of the following:

- technology;
- languages;
- sport;
- arts (visual, performing or media);
- business and enterprise;
- engineering;
- science;
- mathematics and computing.

Specialist schools are expected to work with other schools and the local community, sharing their specialist resources and expertise so that everybody in the community benefits.

Beacon schools

Beacon schools are identified by the DfES as among the best performing schools in the country, with examples of successful practice worth sharing with other schools. Beacon schools are given additional resources to work closely with other schools to share best practice and drive innovation. They are expected to be at the heart of professional learning communities, facilitating networks in order that best practice is shared widely. In September 2002, there were 1,150 Beacon schools in England.

Training schools

Training schools are funded to facilitate networks of schools and teacher training institutions, and help to develop and implement initial teacher training.

Academies

Academies are publicly funded independent schools, which will be state-of-the-art, all-ability specialist schools established by sponsors from business, faith or voluntary groups working with partners from the local community. Sponsors and the Department for Education and Skills provide the capital costs for an academy with running costs met in full by the Department.

Faith schools

Many faith schools are within the state sector, although some are fee-paying. They prefer teachers and pupils of that faith, although they vary in how strict they are about this. Adverts often say something like: 'Applications are welcome from Catholics and other teachers who feel they can make an active contribution to the aims, values and activities of the school.'

Church of England and Catholic schools are either Voluntary Aided (VA) or Voluntary Controlled (VC), depending on the level of autonomy they have opted for. The LEA is the employer and the admissions authority in Voluntary Controlled schools. The governing body is the employer and the admissions authority in VA schools.

The independent sector

The first thing you need to consider is whether you should go into the independent sector. Figure 5.1 lists advantages and disadvantages. Many independent schools are very good but some are appalling. There is still some mistrust and prejudice between the maintained and private sectors and limited movement between the two, so you need to be aware that you may find it hard to get a job in a state school if you start in an independent. You should certainly check that the independent school teaches the National Curriculum in the same way as a state school – and that it keeps up to date with national developments. Some independents can be rather traditional and conservative, and you don't want that to hinder your development as a teacher.

Induction is optional in the independent sector, though most offer and encourage it, but you need to complete induction in order to be able to teach in a state school in England in the future. More importantly, induction will help you through your first year and make you a better teacher so it's important to undergo it as soon as possible – for your and your pupils' sakes. However, the very fact that it is optional causes problems:

From the *TES forum*

'I've found a reception job in a prep school. If I do induction there the head says that I'll have to guarantee to stay for three years to make the financial investment worthwhile – and if I leave before that time I'll have to reimburse them about £500.'

Independent schools don't get the DfES funding (of at least £3,000 a year per NQT), but still have to provide the 90 per cent timetable and all elements of support, monitoring and assessment if they are fulfilling the regulations. This can be expensive, but your school will be saving money on your salary as you'll be cheaper than an experienced teacher. By the way, look at what pay they're offering: independent schools don't have to stick to national pay scales.

Advantages	Disadvantages
Pupils may be better behaved and motivated	Different sort of pupils, socio-economically
Parents may be more supportive	Parental pressure can be great
Smaller classes	Generally fewer opportunities for Continuing Professional Development (CPD)
Not constrained by LEA and DfES bureaucracy	No automatic network with schools and advisers in the LEA, particularly to help if things go wrong in your induction year
Don't have to teach the national curriculum and the national strategies	Teaching and curriculum may be more conservative; they don't get DfES etc publications and resources automatically
More opportunity to coach sports teams	More extra-curricular activities expected
Longer holidays	Longer working day and Saturday classes
	No nationally agreed pay scale
	Union activity is unusual

Figure 5.1   Teaching in independent schools

Supply teaching

Thinking about supply? Tempted by the seductive day rate, the lack of planning, marking and assessing, or the going home at the same time as the kids and without giving another thought to the job? Well, you need to think a few things through.

The pay sounds good. One hears of supplies costing £200 a day, but this figure is what agencies get. You'll get just a fraction of that and you won't be entitled to sick pay, holidays, pension or paid leave. And even if you work for all the 190 school days in a year (which would be unusual), you'll still need money to support you for 365 days. Supply agencies are not charities – they're businesses that make profit and capitalise on staffing crises in schools by putting their prices up. Some are more exploitative than others, so shop around.

The workload is potentially lighter. Not having to write plans, reports and assessments may seem like nirvana after teaching practice, but again there are drawbacks. You'll be expected to follow the planning left for you by class teachers. Gone are the days when you could turn up with winning lessons from your own private repertoire. Working from a plan that isn't yours can be hard, so inevitably lessons don't go so well and you'll rarely get the buzz that comes from successful teaching. If you're in a school for any length of time, you'll be expected to slot into the same level of planning, assessment and reporting as permanent staff, so the workload will become comparable with theirs.

You may be scared at the thought of having to be responsible for the education of a whole class of children. This is a perfectly common feeling, which is probably made a whole lot worse by thinking about it too much. Although not accountable for a whole year's worth, you'll still be responsible for children's well-being and education on every day that you work – and that can be hard in a supply teacher role.

Some people do supply because they can't face the thought of having to cross another mountain, which is what they consider induction (probation in Scotland) to be. It's not a hurdle to be dreaded. You'll have a reduced timetable and someone in charge of supporting, monitoring and assessing you, which is very reassuring. However, supply teachers on induction can be neglected.

From the **TES forum**

'I did two induction terms on supply. No paperwork at all was completed in the first term, no lessons were formally evaluated and I had no NQT meetings in the whole time I was there.'

In England, there are specific rules for NQTs on supply, but some agencies don't make them very clear. Remember these two rules: 1) You can only do short-term supply for four calendar terms starting from your first day's work. After that you must get a post where you can get induction, otherwise you would not be allowed to teach. 2) If you're going to be in a school for a term, you must be on induction and the school has to support, monitor and assess you as it would any other newly qualified teacher. You are entitled to 10 per cent reduced timetable, which the local education authority funds. Make sure you know your rights and gently remind people about their responsibilities.

Agencies vary greatly in terms of the support they give. There are many that will ignore the fact that you are newly qualified and not even tell the school to which they are sending you. Some offer what they call induction, which is actually aimed mostly at teachers from abroad. A few look after NQTs, find them a term's position and offer some training. The fees that agencies pay you and the support they give vary enormously so it's worth shopping around and registering with several, if you decide to do supply.

Supply has pros and cons: with short-term jobs you get to see a variety of schools and practices and you gain a lot of classroom teaching experience very quickly – a real baptism of fire. Doing supply is tough for an experienced teacher, so the odds are stacked against an NQT succeeding. Controlling children you don't know, who see a supply teacher as fair game, and in a school with unfamiliar systems, is hard – and teaching them something worthwhile may be impossible. So try to get a settled job as soon as possible so that you can get the induction support you need.

Moving between primary, secondary and special

Once you have qualified teacher status you can teach in any sort of school, in theory. Every year there are people who trained to teach secondary who decide that they really want to work in primary or vice versa, and those who want to work in special schools. Although these are options, it makes most sense to gain experience in the sort of school that you have experience and training in.

Swapping between different sorts of school is not easy, and best done when you have more experience under your belt. Each is a big leap, even on the amount of subject knowledge you'll need to teach confidently, to say nothing of the different ways of working. It will obviously be harder to get a job in primary if you are trained to teach secondary and vice versa, because you'll be competing with people who have greater knowledge and experience than you. Primary schools will be looking for someone to teach the whole curriculum. They might feel tempted by someone who is a maths or English specialist but are unlikely to do so by someone with French and German. Secondary schools want people who can teach one subject to GCSE if not A level. There are a few conversion courses but experienced teachers are more likely to get places than NQTs who might be deemed to be running away from something. For instance, if you have problems controlling secondary pupils you'll probably find primary even harder.

It's risky to do the move in your induction year as you'll have to meet all the QTS and induction standards, just the same as someone who has undergone training in that age phase. For most people, meeting the QTS standards again is no problem, but for you it will be, as your training experience will be so different from your work. Remember, if you fail to meet the standards after three terms you'll be deregistered from the GTC and never allowed to teach in the maintained sector again. The fact that you're doing induction in a different sort of school to that which you were trained for would not be grounds for appeal if you chose that path.

You can do induction in a special school, and a small number of people do so, but remember that you have your whole career in which to specialise. There are plenty of children with special needs in mainstream schools and the experience of teaching children with the full range of abilities will be invaluable whatever you eventually decide to do. Teaching effectively in a special school requires a great deal. Most people go into them having developed their skills and gained experience in mainstream, which is why there is no initial teaching qualification for special education. It is also easier to go from a mainstream to special school than vice versa. So, for all these reasons, think carefully about going straight into special education. Perhaps spend a few years in mainstream – you'll be classed as experienced then, and be a better proposition for employers.

Deciding what sort of school will suit you

Having considered the whole gamut of big options, think about what sort of a school would suit you. Every time you visit a school and spend time in a classroom and in the playground, take a good look at what you see around you. It will help you work out the kind of school you want to work in.

Look out for the following:

● What kind of relationship is there between pupils and staff – is it formal or informal? Which do you feel more comfortable with?

- Behaviour management policies – are they positive enough? Are they too liberal and lacking in discipline? Different policies suit different schools. What do you feel comfortable with?
- The balance between academic progress and pastoral priorities.
- Staff workload – what sort of hours are teachers working and do they seem happy about workload?
- Staff professional development – how much is there?
- The leadership of the school – every head has their own style. Make mental notes of the style of headteacher you like to work for. The same goes for senior management and departmental heads.
- The other teachers – the staffroom tells you a lot about a school. Are they laughing at the antics of a notorious child, swapping anecdotes, groaning at the latest round of paperwork or what was said about teachers on Radio 4 this morning? Or are their heads stuck in marking books, ignoring each other? More importantly, is there conversation that involves life outside of school? Do they make you pay 10p for a cup of coffee or does someone offer you a choice of biscuits? Is there gossiping about colleagues behind their backs?

These little things tell you a great deal about the character of the school. Different teachers suit different schools. What doesn't feel right for you is a joy to another. And vice versa, of course. The difficulty is deciding what is right for you.

Where to look for a job

You can begin to get a feel for the jobs market even before you decide to apply. Read the *TES* jobs pages or visit www.jobs.tes.co.uk every week to get an idea of the kinds of teaching jobs going for your age range and your specialist subject. Is there a demand in the part of the country where you'd like to teach? If not, where are they? Don't panic unduly. There will be lots more jobs advertised after the end of May, the cut-off date for people to hand in their notice.

Read the jobs pages regularly and you'll get to know the 'ad speak'; a 'challenging' school might be right up your street or it could be your idea of hell. Choose somewhere where you can make the most of your induction year. Concentrate on jobs that ask for a class teacher or main pay scale posts (MPS), which are sometimes referred to as CPS, common pay spine or TPS, teachers' pay scale. The salary scales are explained later in this chapter. You don't want to go for anything with a plus sign such as +1. They are for people with management responsibility, not new teachers.

Jobs that are suitable for newly qualified teachers will often say so. If an advert doesn't specify this, but the post seems to be appropriate for you, give the school a ring and ask. Some schools and or areas within an LEA offer relocation and rent and mortgage subsidies. Bear in mind that these incentives are there because they find it hard to get teachers – there's no such thing as a free lunch. Get a feel for their staff turnover. A school with frequent ads probably has a high turnover. This could mean quick promotion for you, but it's more likely to mean an unstable and unhappy working environment. There are many places where you might find out about a job:

- *National newspapers and their Web sites.* The *TES* is the biggest and most established. It's published every Friday. The *Independent* and The *Guardian* have a smaller number of adverts. If you want to work in a school that subscribes to a particular faith, read the job adverts in that denomination's newspaper.
- *The Times Educational Supplement Web site.* If you register on the *TES* jobs section you can get an e-mail or a text message telling you as soon as a job fitting your requirements is advertised – www.jobs.tes.co.uk. You can choose from:
  - The Early Bird alerts. These let you know about jobs as soon as they are advertised so you can check the *TES* newspaper for details on Friday.
  - The online alerts. These allow you to view jobs online at www.tesjobs.co.uk the following Monday. You either click on a link (for e-mail alerts) or are given a special input code (for text message/SMS alerts).
  - Saving a set of search criteria so you can easily find all jobs matching your requirements.
- *LEA jobs bulletins (paper and Web site).* Many schools advertise locally as well as, or before, doing so nationally. You'll need to register direct with the Human Resources/Personnel department

or Recruitment Strategy Manager to get sent these. You may be asked for an SAE. However, not all schools in an LEA will use this service so keep an eye on national adverts too.

- *LEA pools*. Many LEAs use a pool system for new nursery and primary teachers and some for secondary NQTs. They vary – some LEAs put you through a rigorous interview process, others just add your details to a database so schools can select candidates for interview. Some just keep all the application forms in a box for headteachers to look at. The disadvantage is that the school chooses you rather than you choosing the school, but you can turn offers down and you'll be returned to the pool until you're fished out by the next school that's interested in you. LEA pools mostly advertise in the January issue of *First Appointments*, a *TES* supplement that comes free with the paper once a term. Some will even advertise in the October issue.

- *Informally*. Some jobs aren't advertised. Vacancies are often filled by people who someone at the school knows or has heard of. This is the hardest circle to break into. Many schools will give jobs to people who have done teaching practices with them. Schools also pass information about good trainees they've come across, so it's really important to make good impressions with all your dealings with staff in school. Headteachers aren't necessarily looking for someone who is a brilliant teacher, but someone who takes advice, makes progress, is enthusiastic and gets on with people.

- *Sending CV to schools*. It may be worth sending your CV with an accompanying letter to schools that you fancy working in. This isn't common practice but I've known some people who have got jobs this way. Fiona Flynn's (2001) handy booklet *Get Your First Job* has some useful examples of CVs.

The next chapter looks at what to do when you've found a job that you like.

Getting a job

When you've found a job you like the look of you need to act fast. Most applications have to be in within two weeks of the advert, and interviews are held about a week later. The first step is to ring for an application form and information about the job. Do this straight away – don't delay. For instance, the *TES* comes out on Fridays. You'll need to read it in the morning and ring for an application pack at lunchtime. With luck it will get posted at the end of that day, so you'll probably receive it on Monday or Tuesday. However, you can see how you can lose precious time if you don't request an application until the following week.

Finding out more

Once you've requested the application form, do some detective work. If you found the job ad in the *TES* you can look at a map on its Web site or www.schoolsdirectory.com. Is your journey going to be long and stressful or are the pupils likely to be rather too close to your home for comfort? Ask around – teaching is an 'incestuous' profession and you're bound to find someone who knows about the school. Where is it placed in the league tables? Check out http://www.dfes.gov.uk/performancetables.

You should also read the latest OFSTED report via the *TES* site or try www.ofsted.gov.uk. Look at the date of the report. If it's four or more years old the school may be due for another – do you want to be involved with that? The summary pages are the most useful in getting an overall picture. OFSTED (2000) uses a seven-point grading system, so the words 'good', 'excellent' are used very precisely, so translate what they write to get an accurate picture:

1. excellent;
2. very good;
3. good;
4. satisfactory, sound;
5. unsatisfactory;
6. poor;
7. very poor.

Similarly the standards that pupils are reaching are described on a five-point scale, A–E:

A. well above average;
B. above average;
C. average;
D. below average;
E. well below average.

Look out for the sections on Pupils' Attitudes and Values as well as Leadership and Management – a poorly managed school will be frustrating to work in.

The application form

There are some useful tips about applications in the *TES* booklet *Get Your First Job* (Flynn, 2001). As soon as you get your application form, photocopy it at least twice. You need to perfect a rough copy before you complete the real form. Read through it to see the information it requires. Check the closing date and make sure you have plenty of time to contact referees, draft the form, write the personal statement, complete the form, check it and post it with plenty of time for them to receive it. The first application form you fill in will take a long time! Follow any instructions about sending photocopies, using black ink and deadlines (these will be stuck to). Don't send a CV with your form unless you're asked to – you will have provided the information they want. Write neatly, use a black pen and make sure it doesn't smudge.

Referees

How many referees does it ask for? Normally you need to name two, so people tend to use their college tutor and the headteacher of the most recent teaching practice school. Remember to ask people's permission to put their names as referees and let them know when the closing date for applications and when interviews might be. This will give them an idea of when they'll get the reference request so that they can schedule the writing of it. Often schools expect a quick turn around, and this puts referees under pressure, so the more you can do to ease this the better. Check what contact details you should put on the form – sometimes college tutors prefer to have requests faxed to them via an administrator for speed. Send them a copy of your application form so that they can see what you have written about, decide what needs reinforcing, and what they can mention that you've left out.

Your personal statement

If the form provides space for a personal statement, word-process that on a separate sheet and indicate on the form that it's attached. Your personal statement should be written specifically for each job you apply for, but it's good to prepare a general one that you can amend accordingly. If you're applying to an LEA pool, refer to the named LEA rather than the school. It will be used to assess whether you meet the person specification part of the job description, so pay special attention to this when you're drafting it. There are two examples of a personal statement on the *TES* Web site (www.tes.co.uk/nqt). What do you think of them?

Your personal statement needs to convey that you meet the person specification for the job they are recruiting for. Jot down examples of how you meet each part of the person specification.

You'll find that there are many examples that fit different parts so you need to decide which to use where.

Give examples of how you meet the specification. For instance, 'I have a clear understanding of the literacy and numeracy strategies' says little. Show how you have gained the skills and knowledge through a practical example such as this one from a personal statement on the New Teacher section of the *TES* Web site:

> During my school experience I was able to start to develop and use skills that are necessary to be an effective classroom teacher. I used a range of teaching methods, including discussions, games, collaborative activities and the individual focused tasks. I also made my own resources to help make the lessons interesting and relevant to the children. I tried to motivate and enthuse the children in their work by activities having positive outcomes and celebrating their achievements. I also defined specific learning intentions for each lesson. These factors all contributed to the establishment of a rich and purposeful learning environment. I also listened to and respected the children's thoughts and ideas, and provided support for those who required it, to help the children feel confident, positive and safe within the classroom environment. (www.tes.co.uk/nqt)

When structuring your writing think of how to be helpful to the reader. Use the same headings or order as in the person specification. Express yourself with care. Don't use too much jargon. Be relevant and concise, and don't include anything you can't back up at interview. If it's not on the person specification then it's not likely to be relevant. Address any problematic issues (poor qualifications, gaps in employment) that the reader is likely to have picked up in reading the information parts of the application form. Try to turn things to advantage.

Your personal statement should cover no more than two sides of A4 and it should be word-processed – it's easier to read and looks professional. Proofread it, then get someone else to check it… and then check it again! I can't emphasise enough how off-putting any spelling or grammatical errors are in an application form. Read it out loud to yourself; unlike a CV, your personal statement is prose and it needs to read well. It will be this, more than the rest of your application form, that gets you that interview.

Finally, keep a photocopy and read it again just before your interview. Attach a word-processed covering letter saying where you saw the ad, that your personal statement is attached, that you are newly qualified and that you look forward to discussing your application with them.

You should hear whether you've been shortlisted after a week or two, though there is much anecdotal evidence that this does not always happen.

> **From the TES forum**
>
> 'Usually, a couple of weeks' silence signals that you have not been shortlisted. A month-long pause is enough to let you know that all hope is gone. But your failure is compounded by a lack of manners on the part of the school that refuses to write to say you have been unsuccessful.'

Interviews

As soon as you are offered an interview you'll need to prepare. Time will be short. Try to visit the school before the interview even if you weren't able to do so before you applied. This gives you a huge insight about what is being looked for. Remember, though, that you're being judged even on an informal tour. Try to speak casually to any NQTs to find out if they're happy and that they've been treated well.

Plan your journey with care, leaving room for the unexpected, using Web sites such as http://journeyplanner.tfl.gov.uk/. Not all schools will pay for travel and accommodation for long-distance applicants, so ask before the interview whether they reimburse or contribute to expenses. Some schools in far-flung parts put all candidates up in a hotel the night before. All these little touches give you an insight into what sort of organisation you're going to.

Appearance is really important. You've got to feel good, and look the part. Wear smart clothes, but make sure you'll be comfortable. Shoes can be a real problem if you're on your feet all day. Go for a reasonably professional look but jazz it up with interesting jewellery or a tie to express your personality. Smell is important, too – don't go in reeking of cigarettes or strong scent. Have emergency paracetamol, tissues, and mints. If you're wearing tights, pack a spare pair.

Eat breakfast and turn off that mobile as soon as you get to the school. There is nothing worse than a rumbling belly or a jolly ringtone during an interview.

Take a file with your application form and statement, a portfolio of work from teaching practice (in case you get a chance to show them), and a copy of the most recent *TES*. You can read this while waiting. It will make you look professional and may come in handy in answering a question or two.

Possible interview formats

Interviews vary in how formal they are and how long they last. This would be a question to ask when you phone to accept the interview. If you're going via the pool system you might be interviewed by an LEA adviser, headteacher and someone from Human Resources. If you're being interviewed by a school, the interview could take any number of forms – it just depends on the school, how well organised they are, how proactive their governors are, how many applicants they've got and how short-staffed they might be on the day. It's usually the headteacher, one or two governors and a head of department or other member of staff. I've even known people who have thought they were having a pleasant little chat, only to be told that they have the job – the interview was so informal.

Interviews can take place over a whole day, with all shortlisted candidates together. These may include experienced teachers and internal candidates. Don't be intimidated. Tell yourself you're good, enthusiastic – and cheap! You're likely to get a tour of the school, maybe a group interview/discussion, hopefully lunch, and, if you're there for a whole day, you'll probably be asked to teach a class, observed by some or all of the interviewing panel. You'll then be interviewed individually. You may be asked to wait until they've made their mind up, in which case you'll probably have to sit in the staffroom with the other candidates until one is called in and offered the job. It really is grim.

You're on show all day long. Be friendly and relaxed with any other candidates. If you meet pupils or teachers, ask them about work they're doing and show that you're interested. Look at displays, through classroom doors, the way the pupils and staff conduct themselves. Most importantly, find complimentary things to say about what you see – a little flattery goes a long way. And ask yourself: can you imagine yourself working in this school?

Some schools think up challenging activities for you to do as part of the interview as this posting to the New Teacher Forum shows:

From the *TES forum*

'I was interviewed for a KS1 one-year temporary post, NQT preferred. The school wanted a music specialist – I had made it clear I was not, but had an interest. In groups of four we were given 15 minutes to prepare a 10-minute talk on the benefits of music in the curriculum. We then had to write half a term's planning of a musical topic in 35 minutes, linking it to all the other areas of the curriculum with no literature or national curriculum to refer to.'

Teaching at the interview

Teaching at the interview is ghastly. It's a ridiculous expectation of someone who has yet to complete a teacher training course and isn't yet qualified. Still, you need to be prepared.

Consider what the interviewers are looking for, and plan to give them what they want. Think about how you can show that you're professional, have a rapport with children and manage them well, are enthusiastic, plan well, use effective teaching strategies, and reflect on learning and teaching. Give the interviewers a word-processed copy of your plan – check for spelling errors. Make sure it has a clear learning objective, some useful motivating activities, and clear differentiation. Keep the lesson simple and do it well. Bring your own (or borrowed) resources rather than assuming that the classroom will have them. Think of questions for the very able and for those with special needs. Make sure your behaviour management is as good as possible. Make lots of eye contact with the children, smile, and use praise to reinforce the behaviour you want. Act confidently, even if you're terrified.

Afterwards, reflect on the lesson honestly and intelligently showing that you can assess children's answers, and think of ways to improve your teaching. No one expects you to be perfect, but your interviewers want to see that you're enthusiastic, and can approach and reflect on unfamiliar situations with verve. Oh, and be modest when it goes superbly – they are lovely children aren't they?

Interview tips

- Relax – I know it's hard but breathe deeply, wriggle your toes or do whatever works for you.
- Consider questions before answering and don't be frightened of a few seconds' silence – it's better than gabbling nervously.
- Be reflective – if they raise a weakness, or ask you about something you're weak on, turn it into a positive – give an example of how you picked up an unfamiliar subject quickly, or how a disastrous teaching experience taught you valuable lessons in needing to be flexible/using positive behaviour management/keeping records and so on.
- Make eye contact with whoever is asking you a question and make sure you address each member of the panel during the course of the interview, even the governor who makes notes but says nothing throughout.
- If you're stumped on a question, smile, and ask them to repeat it.
- Be enthusiastic – no one expects a new teacher to be perfect; they can expect you to be enthusiastic, prepared to ride a steep learning curve, to reflect and improve and to approach unfamiliar situations with intelligence.

You're likely to be asked questions along these lines:

- Why do you want to work in this school?
- What makes a good classroom?
- Describe a lesson you've taught that went well.
- How would you handle some difficult behaviour? (They'll give you an example.)
- Tell us about an aspect of your teaching practice you described in your statement.
- How would you ensure that all children were treated equally in your class? Bear in mind gender, race, academic ability and language acquisition.
- How would you like to work with parents?
- How do you approach planning and assessment?
- How do you exploit opportunities for literacy and numeracy in your subject?

- How do you plan to keep up to date in your specialist subject?
- Would you accept the job if it was offered to you?

You can plan answers to these sorts of questions, thinking of examples from your experience that you can use to bring yourself to life. For instance, when asked about how you'd manage some difficult behaviour, refer to a real example of something you've experienced or observed. You'll be asked about your experiences on teaching practice, so have relevant anecdotes to hand on all the issues listed above.

You'll be asked if you have any questions. You do and will have written them down, if you want to come across as bright and proactive. Ask about the school's professional development for teachers and induction support for NQTs, their behaviour management policy, or something specific to the department you'll be working in. If your questions have been answered during the course of the day/interview, then smile and explain what your questions were and that they've been answered, thank you.

You're offered the job

You will usually be offered the job on the day, after everyone else has been interviewed, or a day or two afterwards. The school will expect you to accept straight away. Say you'll accept, *subject to a satisfactory contract and salary*. Remember that phrase, say it again and again in your head: *subject to a satisfactory contract and salary*. The school should be clear about whether the contract is permanent or temporary and about the salary it is offering you, along with arrangements for your induction. If it is not, check you're happy before you formally accept in writing to the school.

From the **TES forum**

'Asking prospective teachers, who are dazed and wrung out by the interview process, to make an instant decision is unfair and unnecessary. I can think of no commercial industry that would get away with such a practice. That teaching has got away with its arcane appointments system for so long is amazing.'

Rejecting an offer

If you decide not to accept the job, be gracious and reject the offer as quickly as possible. You should always treat a school as you would like to be treated yourself. It's not professional to accept a job offer and then change your mind for a better offer, unless you have a good reason such as a sudden change in domestic arrangements. If you have to do this, let them know as quickly as possible, in writing, and explain the reasons why. Bad behaviour has a way of coming back to haunt you.

Being rejected

From the *TES forum*

'I'm an NQT currently working as a supply teacher as I can't get a full-time job. After interviews the feedback I generally get is that I am a "strong candidate" and should have no problems in securing a post in the near future. This is after I have been told that the post has been given to an "outstanding candidate" or someone with "more experience".'

Not getting a job offer is a fact of life for most of us at some point in our careers, so don't take it to heart. This is the time to see an interview as good practice for the next one. Make the most of it as a learning experience. Reflect on what you did well and think about what you can improve on the next time. When you've had a few interviews you can see that the questions are along similar lines. Rack your memory and note down all the questions you can remember being asked. Then you can practise getting the perfect answer to questions on behaviour management, equal opportunities, etc. Don't forget to pepper your answers with real-life examples to bring your responses to life. Come across as enthusiastic and keen to learn. That can more than make up for a lack of experience.

Though it's painful, do ask for feedback so that you can learn from the experience. The bearer of this bad news may not be able to offer this immediately, in which case ask if you can have 10 minutes of their time in the near future. If you're told in writing, ring the school and ask if a member of the panel could call you at a time convenient to them.

You need to persevere in the job hunt. If you don't get a job for the start of term do supply. This will give you rich experience to draw on in future interviews, and is a great way of getting to know about jobs that are coming up. It also gets your name about so that you apply for jobs with a good reputation to back up your assertions.

Contracts

There has been a range of problems with contracts:

- not being given a written contract or job description;
- being given a temporary one;
- being expected to do a different job to the one described in the advert;
- not being given the fair number of points on the salary scale;
- accepting a job without realising that any of the above would be issues.

Over a third of NQTs are given temporary contracts (Totterdell *et al*, 2002), for no good reason. This results in insecurity, inequality and low status. Clearly, a large number of schools are discriminating against new teachers. One school rarely renews NQTs' one-year contracts, preferring to get a new lot of cheap labour each year so that it can keep its salary budgets down: a continuous supply of cannon fodder. Temporary contracts are not good and you should apply for permanent posts, unless you have very little option and you really, really want the job.

There are times when you might agree to something that you later regret, like this person from the New Teacher Forum:

Top tip!

Q: 'I applied for a Key Stage One job, but at the interview I was asked if I would consider Foundation stage – only too keen, I agreed! I was offered the job and accepted. I've since been told the position is to be the nursery teacher. I have no experience in the nursery and I am now extremely worried about my induction year.

Ideally I would like to get a KS1 position at a different school but where do I stand as I have already verbally accepted the job?'

A: You've been put in an uncomfortable position, but need to solve the problem quickly before it affects you and the school too much. A verbal agreement is as legally binding as a written one. Having said that, a school won't want you to be unhappy and can't realistically do much about you reneging on it. Anyway, much of the fault lies with the school in not being clear about the post, so I think you should explain your concerns to the head as soon as possible, so that both of you have time to resolve the situation. Here are some things to say. The organisation and management of children, staff and parents requires a high level of maturity, experience and skill, which you do not have. While you would be interested in such a challenge in the future, you feel that such a role would be too much for you in your induction year and thus would require the school to provide a great deal of support. You thought you were being interviewed for a Key Stage 1 job, and really feel that this is where your strength lies. Ask whether there is any possibility that you could teach at KS1 (I'm sure teachers could be reallocated classes). If there isn't, say that though you really want to work at the school you regret that you will have to look elsewhere.

seven

Starting the job

- Before you start
- Salary
- Setting up your classroom
- Parents

Before you start

The induction process starts as soon as you are appointed. You should get a job description and contract, and know the arrangements for salary payments, pension contributions and procedures for sick leave. You may be asked to go for a medical. You should be sent documentation to enable you to get a feel for the school. This would include the following, though items might be prioritised or staggered to avoid overload.

Preliminary documentation

- school prospectus;
- staff handbook or something that details things such as how to complete the register, school and playground rules, planning formats;
- teaching staff list – professional and staffroom names, classes taught and responsibilities;
- support staff list – professional and staffroom names and responsibilities;
- administration staff list – professional and staffroom names and responsibilities;
- curriculum policies;
- curriculum schemes of work relevant to your year group;

- other policies (health and safety, child abuse, bullying, etc);
- timetable;
- diary sheet of school events.

The initial visit

Before you start work try to arrange, where possible, to visit the school to familiarise yourself with the environment, colleagues and meet the class(es) that you will be teaching. Ideally, you should leave the school feeling full of enthusiasm, with lots of information and secure in the knowledge that you will be supported. Careful planning will ensure that you get the most out of the visit. Ask whether all the people you think you'll want to talk to will be available. Everyone will be busy and unlikely to be able to spare you much time so write a list of all the things you want to know and tick them off when you've found the answer. Make another list of items that you want to come away with.

I have, however, known people to return from these visits so worried that they speak of not signing contracts. Their impressions of the school gained at interview have been contradicted by talking to jaded teachers, and seeing pupils behaving badly. As a result, every year there are one or two NQTs who do not turn up at their school or who leave after the first week. Remember that you're probably seeing the school at its least desirable: at the end of term with exhausted teachers and demob-happy pupils. It will be better at the start of the school year.

Checklist for your initial visit

You should:

- meet the pupils;
- get a feel for the standard of work of the pupils (high, average, and low attainers) that you will be teaching;
- look at records;
- see the classroom;
- look at resources in your classroom;
- look at resources in the school;
- look at the local environment;

- become familiar with routines and procedures;
- meet all teaching, administration and support staff;
- spend some time with key people:
  - the head and deputy;
  - teachers who know the pupils you will be teaching;
  - induction tutor;
  - teachers who you will be planning with;
  - year and/or phase group coordinator or head of department;
  - SENCO;
  - support staff with whom you will be working;
  - premises officer;
  - secretary.

At some time before or during the first week, the induction tutor needs to agree a programme with you based on the CEDP (Career Entry and Development Profile) and your teaching context.

Salary

The information in this section is up to date as I write but is liable to change. It comes from the *School Teachers' Pay and Conditions* document. Keep up to date by looking on http://www.teachernet.gov.uk/pay.

The ordinary classroom jobs suitable for NQTs are on the main pay scale (MPS). Some adverts refer to this by its old name CPS, common pay spine, or teachers' pay scale (TPS). Ignore upper pay scale (UPS). This is what people get when they've reached the top of the main pay scale and have successfully passed the Threshold assessment. The leadership group pay scale is for deputies and senior managers. There are six points on the main pay scale:

Scale from 1 April 2003 £pa

Spine point	£	Inner London £
M1	18,105	21,522
M2	19,536	22,977
M3	21,108	24,573
M4	22,734	26,226
M5	24,525	28,041
M6	26,460	30,000

> ### From the *TES forum*
> 'I completed my NQT year in December so I presumed I'd be moving up a point on the scale in January. My mentor has informed me that I will not rise up the scale until September.'

Teachers normally get one extra point on the main pay scale every year, usually, but not necessarily, every September. Most people start on M1 and after six years will be at the top of the scale. In exceptional cases, teachers can be awarded an extra point on the scale for excellent performance over the previous academic year, so they would go up two points in a year. People on the Fast Track scheme are expected to do so (see Chapter 1). Similarly, the annual point progression can be withheld if the teacher's performance has been unsatisfactory, but again this is rare.

Each school's governing body can (but they don't have to) award additional points for other relevant experience. You'll need to be proactive in asking for this, but there's not much you can do if they don't give you an additional point since it's at the discretion of individual governing bodies. Once awarded, experience points, whether originally mandatory or discretionary, can't be taken away regardless of whether you stay in the same school or get a post in another school.

> ### From the *TES forum*
> 'We were told at uni to negotiate wages if you had experience etc, but I had no chance. I was told that the County worked out salaries and that was it. I didn't know my salary until I started work and I was very disappointed. I have no experience points! I am a mature student, with years of work experience as a classroom assistant. Be very careful!'

You need to be proactive in saying why you should be on a higher scale than the average NQT. Age alone is no reason. Have you had relevant experience? If so, negotiate this when you are offered the job. They can only say no and might say yes – so you have nothing to lose. You'll handle it very professionally, I'm sure, so that you don't look greedy or cheeky!

Allowances

Classroom teachers on the main pay scale can also get allowances. The inner London area allowance is now within a separate scale. This gives people on mainscale an extra £3,500 and an extra £6,000 on the upper pay scale. You'll get £2,247 extra in outer London and £870 in fringe areas.

There are also allowances for management responsibilities, special needs and recruitment and retention. NQTs would normally only be eligible for a recruitment and retention allowance, but it's useful to know about them all.

Management allowances

There are five levels of management allowances that can be awarded to a teacher who 'undertakes significant specified management responsibilities beyond those common to the majority of classroom teachers':

Management 1	£1,638
Management 2	£3,312
Management 3	£5,688
Management 4	£7,833
Management 5	£10,572

NQTs shouldn't be asked to take on management responsibilities, though some people are, with or without an allowance, as the posting to the Forum below illustrates. After your first year you can't refuse to take a subject leader role in primary and may not get any financial recompense, so make the most of it.

Top tip!

Q: 'I recently applied for a position as a music teacher and have been offered the job, as has another candidate who is also just coming up to the end of a PGCE. We were told that because we would both be acting as heads of the music department, we would each get one management point. But we have since been informed that we won't get any management points because, being NQTs, we're not eligible for them.'

A: This is tricky. The school has broken a verbal but legally binding contract, so you would be within your rights to turn down the job. If I were you, I would consider doing so. It sounds as if you'd be expected to do a head of department's job without a management point, and that would be unfair. There's nothing to stop NQTs having a management point, though it would be unusual. The extra money might not compensate for the stress you would perhaps experience. Sharing a position would be hard for experienced teachers, but for two NQTs it would be disastrous.

Under paragraph 26 of the induction circular (DfES, 2000), you are protected from any position that makes 'unreasonable demands'. Clearly, being expected to be a head of department would be unreasonable, whether the job is shared or not. The school's willingness to give this job to two NQTs shows there is no one else to take the role, and perhaps suggests poor leadership and management. This would mean your induction tutor would be someone from outside the music department who may be unable to support you well or judge your work fairly.

Special needs allowances

There are two levels of special needs allowance that are given to classroom teachers in special schools and those teaching designated special classes in mainstream schools:

Special needs 1   £1,674
Special needs 2   £3,312

Recruitment and retention allowances

There are five allowances for recruitment and retention that schools can use if they have problems in getting staff:

Recruitment & retention 1	£1,002
Recruitment & retention 2	£1,971
Recruitment & retention 3	£2,985
Recruitment & retention 4	£4,158
Recruitment & retention 5	£5,415

If you are unqualified

If a school employs you before you get QTS you'll be paid on the unqualified teacher scale. This may be because you're on the Graduate Teacher Programme or are an overseas trained teacher or because you haven't passed all components of your training course.

Scale point £	£pa	Inner London £pa
1	13,266	16,683
2	13,860	17,277
3	14,439	17,856
4	15,039	18,456
5	15,645	19,062
6	16,227	19,644
7	16,824	20,241
8	18,216	21,633
9	19,794	23,211
10	20,979	24,396

What you'll actually get paid

From the *TES forum*

'I'm not overly concerned about actually getting a job, but how much money I'll have if I get one. We have been told horror stories about tax, national insurance, union memberships, pensions, superannuation, teachers' councils etc. What do we have to pay and what is optional?' Jill

Jill is not alone in wondering exactly how much will be in her pay packet. You will have deductions for:

* tax – have to pay;
* National Insurance – have to pay;
* pension (also called superannuation) – strongly advised to pay;
* General Teaching Council – have to pay £33 a year in England;
* union subscription – optional but highly advisable.

All but the lowest paid work incurs National Insurance deductions. These build up towards your state pension and give you rights to statutory sick pay and other welfare benefits. You pay tax on any money earned over your Personal Allowance of approximately £4,500 per annum. The next £1,880 earned after this are taxed at 10 per cent, then the rest is taxed at 22 per cent. Superannuation is the 6 per cent deducted to fund your Teachers' Pension, which is of the prized final salary type. The employer contributes to it, so it's much better than a Personal Pension. You can also make Additional Voluntary Contributions (AVCs) to boost your pension.

 From the TES forum

'I am on the basic starting wage of £17,595. I get £1,089 a month after deductions for tax, national insurance and pension.'

Repayments on the Teachers' Loan kick in when you've earned over £10,000 in a tax year. That is why you don't have anything deducted in your first two terms of teaching – assuming you start in September.

The English General Teaching Council fee of £33 was a bone of contention when it was brought in so the amount has now been added to the main scale pay rates and is then deducted by the LEA employers from your pay. Union membership is offered at a reduced rate for NQTs and is regarded by most teachers as a necessity. Join all the unions for free while you are a PGCE student and assess which provides the best information and service.

Setting up your classroom

One of the hardest things that you'll have to do as a teacher is also the first – set up the classroom. It really is exciting. You have your own classroom at last!

Try to visit the school at the end of term, before you start. Have a good look around at the classroom you'll be in and what it's got. Look at other rooms and resources in the school. Perhaps draw diagrams and take photos because things will look very different at the start of the school year. You really need to go into school in the last week of the holiday before you start. Find out when the building will be open and teachers allowed in. You'll probably be confronted with a pile of furniture in the middle of the room – a ghastly sight! Don't panic but think about how other classrooms you've been in have been arranged – dig out those diagrams and photos from teaching practice. The physical environment is crucial, but a well-arranged and organised room needs planning, physical effort and time.

The position of electrical sockets will determine where you put computers, tape recorders and overhead projectors. When you've got these in position you can build up the rest of the room. Make sure you've got a desk to work at (don't ruin your back by crouching over the children's tables after school) and shelves to store your files, etc. A lockable drawer or cupboard is useful for keeping things like money and staple guns.

Top tip!

Q: 'Are teachers' desks a right? Our headteacher insists that desks are unnecessary. He says that good teachers can manage without them.'

A: No, it's not a 'right' but it is standard issue for most teachers. Sorry to sound rude, but your headteacher is talking nonsense and undermining your self-esteem when he or she implies that you're not a good teacher because you want one. If he/she applied the same logic you probably wouldn't have a chair because you never sit down, or a staffroom because you're always in the classroom. Could your headteacher do without a desk? Surely he/she should be out of his or her office leading and managing, and not hiding behind a desk when someone visits. He/she needs to write a letter? Well, he/she can use the secretary's desk.

Do you need to explain that you won't be sitting behind the desk (feet up, drinking coffee) when teaching? What an insult. Where do you work when the children aren't there? You'll damage your back if you try working at the children's tables – and then be off sick. A desk is essential. Where do you keep all your stuff if you haven't got one? Where do you put work to mark, important documents, etc. I'm sure your headteacher wouldn't want you to leave sensitive documents lying around the place – memos about problem pupils or sensitive school issues. How can you be organised without a desk to put things in and on? It's common sense to give teachers the space to work and an area that they can truly call their own.

Furniture

Look at the furniture you've been given. Are there items that you don't need? Often new teachers are given cast-offs. Look around other classrooms to check that you have a fair allocation. Are there enough tables and chairs? Find out the maximum number of children you'll have in the room and then have a couple spare in case of new arrivals, needing to split people up or being sent children from another class. Remember to allow space for moving around and for other adults who might be working in the room, and any equipment for children with special needs.

Think about how you're going to teach when deciding how to arrange the tables. How often do the children work collaboratively in groups? Everyone needs to see you when you're whole-class teaching so where are you going to stand? Where is the whiteboard? Popular arrangements include rows, horseshoes and clusters of fours or sixes. Choose whatever you think is going to work best for you and the children rather than slavishly following what other teachers do.

Nigel Hastings and Karen Chantrey-Wood (2002) found huge benefits to flexible seating arrangements. For instance, Louise has two layouts for her Year 3 class of 26 children. Her basic arrangement is a double horseshoe with tables laid out into a big and small U shape, and a table for a group teaching. This is used for whole-class teaching and paired and individual work. There's sufficient space between the two U shapes for her to move comfortably around and work in front or behind any child. She rearranges the tables for collaborative activities, usually in science, DT and history. They are moved to form five grouped sets. A team of six children does this just before break times and it only takes a minute.

Resources

Have you got everything that you need to teach your age group? Ask your induction tutor for missing items. Organise resources to minimise fuss and wasted time. Everyone should know where they're kept and the procedures for getting things out and putting them away. Think hard about the particularly troublesome things such as:

- things brought from home, packed lunch boxes, bags, PE kits;
- pencils and pens, sharpeners, rubbers, scissors;
- exercise books, worksheets, unfinished work;
- reading folders, homework.

Procedures

Discuss with the children what the rules for the smooth running of the class should be. This is a good activity for the first day of term. Ask everyone (including other adults) in the class if they agree with them. Phrase them positively, perhaps as promises: 'We will listen when an adult is talking.' Display them centrally, perhaps with illustrations. Refer to them continually: 'Well done, you're doing rule 3.'

Think through procedures for moving from the carpet to tables, lining up, going to the toilet, tidying, etc. These need planning, training, practice and reinforcement, particularly for difficult times of the day such as these, chosen from secondary and primary teachers:

- dealing with parents in the mornings;
- giving out and collecting in work;
- registration;
- tidying up;
- carpet time;
- transitions within and between lessons;
- lining up;

- moving around the school;
- after break times;
- just before lunch;
- home time;
- changing reading books;
- drink time;
- changing for PE;
- wet playtimes;
- setting homework.

Don't worry if things don't work straight away. You'll need to adjust the arrangement of the room and procedures so that they work for your class. This takes time and effort, but it's worthwhile. You will be able to teach more effectively and the children will learn more so the classroom will be a happier, more productive place.

Display

The number of bare display boards in your room may fill you with blind panic. Unless they're painted or already covered, ask an assistant to put up backing paper and some posters until the pupils do some displayable work. You may be in a school where support assistants do all the displays for you. Even so, you'll probably need to tell them what you want. Getting ideas for displays can be hard so keep photos of displays, look around the school and in books, and ask others for inspiration. There are always people in school who love display and will be more than happy to help you. In fact, many, including myself, find it a really creative, relaxing and rewarding part of teaching. Ask for help. Here are some tips that NQTs have shared:

- Word-process labels – and keep them on file for the future.
- Laminate labels that can be used again.
- Laminate small labels with pupils' names on for attaching to their work.
- Involve the pupils, eg in writing labels, mounting work, and finding artefacts.
- Incorporate the making of a display into the lesson.
- Pre-cut paper (to be smaller than A4) for pupils to work on so that it can be mounted on A4 paper and not need trimming.

- Have permanent displays that only need occasional adding to (eg, literacy – alphabet, key words).
- Attach some card or a coin to your staple gun so that the staple doesn't go all the way in the board but is slightly raised for easy removal. That way, work, labels and backing paper won't get torn.
- Save artefacts for displays that you are likely to repeat.

Parents

Dealing with parents is challenging because it calls for skills that you probably had little need to develop during teaching practices. Parents/carers can be very difficult to cope with – especially if they know that you are an NQT. You need to fill them with confidence (something that you may not feel) that their child is in safe hands educationally. Parents/carers want to know that you will be fair, not pick on their child, keep order so that their child can get on with their work, and teach well to enable progress to be made. They will also probably expect you to know their child well. Tips for dealing with parents/carers are:

- Look confident.
- Dress appropriately.
- Act particularly professionally and confidently when parents are around.
- In all dealings maintain a quietly assertive, polite and confident manner.
- Maintain a professional distance no matter how well you get to know the parents.
- Be honest though tactful.
- Give clear messages – avoid educational jargon.
- Listen to what they have to say.
- Follow up concerns that they have.
- Do whatever you say you will do.
- Refer significant issues to more senior teachers.

Your school may ask you to keep a record of both formal and informal contacts with parents/carers. This can be used when you initiate contact over problems such as lateness, homework or behaviour, or more positive things such as a particularly good piece of work or improvement in behaviour.

Parents' evenings

Parents' evenings are stressful, even for experienced teachers. Many NQTs find the thought terrifying. Everyone feels the same way and everyone survives. You should get some help from your induction tutor. Someone needs to talk you through your specific school's procedures and to warn you of any parents who are known to be difficult – and the best way to deal with them. Ideally, arrange to sit in on another teacher's interview with a parent to see how they structure it.

You'll feel more confident if you prepare. What is the aim of the consultation? Is it for you to meet parents, or to set targets and discuss progress? Whatever it is make sure that the parents are clear and that you're prepared. Spend some of your 10 per cent reduced timetable getting ready.

Write notes on each child, identifying strengths and areas for development socially and academically (see Figure 7.1). It's useful to ask the children what they think you'll say. Their understanding of how they're doing is essential. Keep the notes on separate pieces of paper so that people can't see what you're going to say about any other children. Check the last written report so that you know what the parents have been told before. You'll probably be reinforcing what has already been said but if you're planning to say something that contradicts previous messages, make sure you have hard evidence to back you up. If you can predict what issues parents might raise, think of some answers. Take care with what you say and how you say it, as it'll all get analysed and talked about afterwards. Be thoroughly professional and tactful: if you think someone's lazy then say that the pupil has not really worked hard this term but that there is still time to turn this around.

Plan the timetable of meetings carefully, giving yourself breaks where possible – but don't rely on having any gaps as you'll probably run over time with some parents. Organise your teaching for the day and the day after to be fairly easy going. You won't have the time or energy to do marking or planning after a parents' evening.

You are being judged as much as the pupils (especially as a new teacher) so make sure your personal presentation does you credit. Bring a spare set of smart clothes to change into and allow time to

Pupil	
Work – strengths	
Illustrative piece of work:	
Work – weaknesses	
Illustrative piece of work:	
Areas to work on	
Social, behaviour and attitude	
Targets	
Parents'/carers' comments	
Date	

Figure 7.1   Notes for parents'/carers' evenings

freshen up. Arrange a table and some adult-sized chairs. Ensure that marking is up to date and everything looks organised, especially any work that is going to be looked at. If you're in primary try to have something from every child on display. Keep anything to hand that you might possibly need, such as examples of work, records and curriculum documents. Lastly, have a supply of drinks and nibbles to keep you going. Try to look confident – even if you don't feel it. Remember that most parents will be nervous too.

Top tip!

Q: 'A parent of a bright child asked me at a parents' evening how his son was getting on and insisted that his son should take GCSE mathematics early. I told him his son was doing extremely well, was well ahead of the rest of the class and most of the work was too easy for him. He wanted to know what I was doing to stretch him and I admitted I didn't have time to produce individual work for him and that my main priority was the other 31 in the group. Was I right to be honest?'

A: If I'd been the parent I wouldn't have been happy. Tell your HoD straight away in case there is fall out and get some help with stretching him. Then let the parent know what action you've taken.

The meeting itself

Make sure that parents know how long they've got with you – this is normally only about 10 minutes but both you and they will want longer. Keep a clock or watch on the table so that you and they can keep to time, although this is very hard to do. You need to manage the time really well – try to be ruthlessly efficient. Trouble will brew if people are kept waiting too long. You can always suggest that parents who need longer make an appointment to see you on another occasion. Work out a structure for the meeting, such as (Bubb, 2001: 71):

> *Introduction*: Hello, you must be X's mum or you've come to talk about X (don't use people's last name unless you're sure of it, can pronounce it and know their title – the potential for offence and wasted time is too great).
>
> *Headline*: X has settled in well and is making progress.
>
> *Strengths* (social and academic): I'm particularly pleased with... (have some work that illustrates your point).
>
> *Area for improvement* (social and academic): However, X still needs to work on... (again, have some illustration).
>
> *Parents' views*: How do you think X is doing? Do you have any concerns? (You could ask this after your headline but you'd risk losing time for your agenda. If you know what they are likely to raise, plan a response. Make a note of their concerns.)
>
> *Parental help*: Could you make sure X practises...
>
> *Conclusion*: (look at watch, stand up, offer hand for shaking) Well, thank you for coming. If you have concerns in the future please let me know.

If you can predict parents who might be difficult, arrange for another member of staff to be around, perhaps bringing you a cup of coffee at a prime time. Have a list of your appointments and tick when you have seen parents. This should stop you getting confused and talking about the wrong child – it has happened!

You'll feel a great sense of achievement when it's over, so celebrate with a glass of something nice in a hot, relaxing bath.

eight

Understanding induction

- Differences between England, Scotland and Wales
- The rules in England
- Roles and responsibilities
- Induction tutors

Becoming a really good teacher is like a long journey. Some parts will be smooth and fast flowing, others stressful and full of traffic jams – but you'll be making progress all the time even if the congestions you meet reduce your speed to only five miles an hour. Induction and all professional development can help you pick up speed in your journey. If you don't take advantage of what it has to offer it won't be the end of the world. You'll make some progress just through experience – but you'll only be travelling slowly. Using all the help available to develop professionally will get you speeding along at a comfortable 30 mph. But beware the temptation to speed or you might crash. You'll burn out or get promoted to positions for which you are insufficiently experienced and credible – and which cause you stress.

Differences between England, Scotland and Wales

The regulations and support covering the first year of teaching vary depending on which country you work in. England has had statutory induction since May 1999, Scotland changed from a two-year to a one-year probationary period in August 2002, and Wales is making induction compulsory from September 2003. Table 8.1

compares the rules for the three countries and the standards that NQTs have to meet in England are below and those for Wales and Scotland are in Appendices 2 and 3 respectively. This chapter concentrates on English regulations but here is some key information about Wales and Scotland.

Scotland

All teachers must be fully registered with the Scottish GTC to get a post in a school. New teachers are given provisional registration and have to do a year's probation and meet the standards for full registration. In response to previous difficulties in finding long-term posts, the period of probation has been reduced from two to one year and those people who finish their training in Scotland are guaranteed a one-year new teaching post. They are allocated to one of the 32 LEAs and then to a school. You can't choose a school. The placement is for one year, but there's no guarantee that people will be able to stay afterwards. Deferment isn't possible, except on such grounds as needing maternity leave. People who trained outside Scotland can do probation if they have a provisional registration with the GTC but they aren't guaranteed a new teacher post.

New teachers are given a very generous 70 per cent timetable – the rest is for professional development, which consists of core experiences that the authorities organise, and individual activities. Each new teacher has a special 'supporter' who has a role similar to the induction tutor in England. This person has half a day each week to meet and observe the new teacher. Assessment forms are completed twice a year. The standards on which new teachers are judged (Appendix 3) cover rather more extensive areas than those in England and build on those standards for Scottish initial training.

Wales

Wales has been slow to make induction statutory, although first-time teachers have been very well looked after in many schools. The induction year is only statutory for all new entrants from September 2003.

The distinctive feature of the proposals in Wales is that induction is seen as part of early professional development over the first three years. This is already in place in Northern Ireland and is also being piloted by some English authorities. NQTs are assessed on induction standards (see Appendix 2). Anyone failing will be given the opportunity to retake induction: this is certainly a softer approach than England's 'zero tolerance of failure'.

	England	Scotland	Wales
First year called	Induction	Probation	Induction
You're known as	NQT	New teacher	NQT
Entry qualifications	Degree + QTS	BEd or Degree + PGCE, not GTP or RTP	Degree + QTS. Speaking Welsh helps but not essential
GCSEs	English and maths C grade+	English lit and lang C grade. Primaries – maths B grade	English and maths C grade+
Arrangements started	May 1999	Aug 2002	Sept 2003
Lead organisation	General Teaching Council for England	General Teaching Council for Scotland	General Teaching Council for Wales
Timetable reduction	10%	30%	10%
Who looks after you	Induction tutor	Supporter	Induction tutor
Time for their job	None	0.1	None
Judged against	Induction standards	The Standard for Full Registration	The End of Induction Standard
Assessment	three times	two times	three times
How to get a job	You find it	You are placed in a school	You find it
Time limit between QTS and induction	None	Have to do probation straight away	None

Table 8.1   The first year – differences between England, Scotland and Wales

The rules in England

England has the most vacancies for NQTs and the most embedded induction arrangements. Induction was made statutory in 1999 (DfES, 2000). Schools are given about £1,000 per term per NQT from the Standards Fund to fund induction. NQTs are protected from 'unreasonable' demands such as curriculum coordination and especially demanding behaviour problems. They have an individualised programme of support, monitoring and assessment from an induction tutor and objectives are set to help meet the standards for the induction period. There are assessment meetings and reports at the end of each of the three terms. For those who don't do well in their first year, the consequences are awful (Emmerson, 2000). People who fail induction in England are never allowed to teach in maintained schools or non-maintained special schools again. They cannot retake induction, and extensions are only allowed in special cases such as more than 30 days' illness. There is an appeal process but this is very stressful. The good news is that since induction became mandatory in May 1999 there have been 56,263 NQTs who have passed their induction, and only 94 who have failed (data provided by the GTCE, 5 December 2002) – so the failure rate is only 0.2 per cent.

The induction period lasts for a school year, which in most cases means that it will start in September and end in July. This is three terms or the equivalent. Thus, if you only work two and a half days a week your induction period will last for six terms. It should start as soon as you start work on a regular timetable for at least a term, even if this is in the middle of a term. The induction circular says that:

> The induction period will combine an individualised programme of monitoring and support, which provides opportunities for NQTs to develop further their knowledge, skills and achievements in relation to the Standards for the award of QTS, with an assessment of their performance. (DfES, 2000: paragraph 4)

The key words are: monitoring, support and assessment. In practice, this means that there is an entitlement for NQTs that should last throughout their induction period. Figure 8.1 (p 126) shows how the support, monitoring and assessment can be balanced over the year.

The induction standards

To complete the induction period satisfactorily, the DfES regulations require an NQT to: 1) meet all the induction standards; and 2) continue to meet the standards for the award of QTS, consistently and with increasing professional competence. To meet these requirements, NQTs need to:

- work with increasing professional competence in areas where, during initial training, it was assumed that they would need the support of an experienced teacher;
- focus on aspects of professional practice that can be better developed during employment as a qualified teacher, and over a longer period of teaching than is available to most trainee teachers during their initial training;
- consolidate and build on what they have already achieved in order to be awarded QTS.

The induction standards (DfES, 2003a)

Professional Values and Practice
They continue to meet the requirements of the Professional Values and Practice section of the Standards for the Award of QTS, and build on these. Specifically, they:

a. seek and use opportunities to work collaboratively with colleagues to raise standards by sharing effective practice in the school.

Knowledge and Understanding
They continue to meet the requirements of the Knowledge and Understanding section of the Standards for the Award of QTS, and build on these. Specifically, they:

b. show a commitment to their professional development by:

- identifying areas in which they need to improve their professional knowledge, understanding and practice in order to teach more effectively in their current post; and
- with support, taking steps to address these needs.

Teaching
They continue to meet the requirements of the Teaching section of the Standards for the Award of QTS, and build on these by demonstrating increasing responsibility and professional

competence in their teaching and when working with other adults, including parents. Specifically, they:

c.   plan effectively to meet the needs of pupils in their classes with special educational needs, with or without statements, and in consultation with the SENCO contribute to the preparation, implementation, monitoring and review of Individual Education Plans or the equivalent;
d.   liaise effectively with parents or carers on pupils' progress and achievements;
e.   work effectively as part of a team and, as appropriate to the post in which they are completing induction, liaise with, deploy, and guide the work of other adults who support pupils' learning;
f.   secure a standard of behaviour that enables pupils to learn, and act to pre-empt and deal with inappropriate behaviour in the context of the behaviour policy of the school.

The NQT entitlement

Some NQTs get more than they are strictly entitled to, but about a fifth do not get all that they should have (Totterdell *et al*, 2002). You're entitled to the following:

1.   a job description that does not make unreasonable demands (see below);
2.   an induction tutor;
3.   meetings with the induction tutor;
4.   the Career Entry and Development Profile – the document that helps provide a bridge from training to the rest of your career – discussed by the NQT and induction tutor;
5.   objectives, informed by the strengths and areas for development identified in the CEDP, to help NQTs improve so that they meet the standards for the induction period;
6.   a 10 per cent reduction in timetable – half a day off a week or the equivalent number of free periods;
7.   a planned programme of how to spend that time, such as observations of other teachers;

8. at least one observation each half-term with oral and written feedback, meaning a minimum of at least six a year;
9. an assessment meeting and report towards the end of each term;
10. procedures for NQTs to air grievances about their induction provision at school and a 'named person' to contact at the Appropriate Body (see below), usually the LEA.

However, there are many confusions about and contraventions of the induction policy. Here are answers to frequently asked questions:

Where can I do statutory induction?
These regulations only apply to England, Guernsey, Jersey, Gibraltar and the Isle of Man. You can't do induction in a school abroad.

Are there any schools in England in which I can't do induction?
Yes, you can't do induction in a Pupil Referral Unit, or a school under special measures unless HMI says you'll be well supported. You can only do it in an independent school if they have an Appropriate Body – the LEA or ISCTIP.

The school says it can't afford to give me 10 per cent release time.
It's a statutory duty of headteachers to give NQTs only a 90 per cent timetable. Your headteacher has no choice in the matter.

My half-day for induction is often cancelled because of staff sickness.
There will inevitably be times when this happens, but your induction time should be protected as far as possible and, if missed, should be made up at some other time.

What happens if I fail induction?
If your head and LEA think that you do not meet the induction standards, you won't be allowed to teach in a maintained school or non-maintained special school in England. However, you can appeal against the decision. You would be able to teach in an independent school, a city technology college, or work as a private tutor. Your qualified teacher status isn't taken away.

Who must complete the statutory induction period?
Everyone who qualified after May 1999 has to complete an induction period to work in state schools in England. If you received

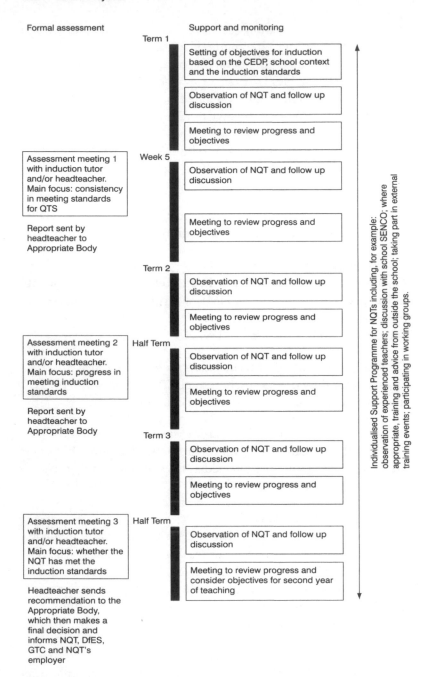

Figure 8.1   Overview of the induction process (TTA, 2002a: 6)

your QTS before 1999 but have not taught, you'll still be called an NQT but you won't have to pass the induction standards.

Is there a time limit between qualifying and starting induction?
No. You can also take a break after the first or second of the three terms in the induction period, if you need one. The only things that have a time limit are supply work, Golden Hellos and the Repayment of Teacher Loans scheme.

Everyone says I'm doing well, so my induction has fizzled out.
Induction is statutory for all NQTs. Even the very successful have the right to be challenged so they become even more effective teachers. Be proactive in asking for meetings and observations.

The school is in crisis – priorities are elsewhere, not on us.
It will be particularly hard to complain to the head and LEA in this situation, but all the more important. If you are not getting the support you need, you won't teach effectively and the children's learning will suffer further.

Roles and responsibilities

It's essential that everyone is clear about roles and responsibilities. The TTA outlines the roles clearly in the booklet *Supporting Induction for Newly Qualified Teachers. Part 1: Overview* (TTA, 2002a). You should take an active role in all aspects of the induction process:

- Make your CEDP available to the school, and work with your induction tutor to use the CEDP and the induction standards as a basis for setting objectives for professional development and devising an action plan.
- Take part in planning your induction programme, including the identification and reviewing of objectives.
- Engage fully in the programme of monitoring, support and assessment that is agreed with the induction tutor, taking increasing responsibility for your professional development as the induction period progresses.
- Be familiar with the induction standards, monitor your own

work in relation to them and contribute to the collection of evidence towards your formal assessment.

- Raise any concerns you have about the content and/or delivery of your induction programme. (TTA, 2002a: 8)

Being aware of your rights will help you in any area of concern. Use this book, the induction circular (DfES, 2000) and the TTA *Supporting Induction* booklets (TTA, 2002a) to back up any points that you need to make. Knowing the Appropriate Body, headteacher and induction tutor's responsibilities will also help you.

The Appropriate Body

Schools need to have an Appropriate Body to which they send reports and that has a quality assurance role. All LEAs act as Appropriate Bodies. In independent schools, the Appropriate Body will be either the LEA for the area in which the school is situated or the Independent Schools Council Teacher Induction Panel (ISCTIP). The induction circular outlines what is expected of Appropriate Bodies. Their specific statutory duties are:

- ensuring that headteachers and governing bodies are aware of and capable of meeting their responsibilities for monitoring, support and guidance (paragraph 19);
- ensuring headteachers are capable of undertaking rigorous and fair assessments of NQTs (paragraph 19);
- making the final decision about whether an NQT meets the standards for the completion of the induction period and communicating their decision to NQTs, schools and the DfES/GTC (paragraph 87);
- keeping records and assessment reports on NQTs (paragraph 21);
- providing a named person for NQTs to contact if they are unhappy with schools' support, monitoring and assessment (paragraph 32);
- extending the induction period in exceptional circumstances (paragraph 82);
- ensuring that schools with NQTs get earmarked funding (paragraph 101).

(DfES, 2000)

It must also identify a named contact on induction matters, with whom NQTs may raise issues about their induction programme where they cannot be resolved satisfactorily within the school. So, what can new teachers do when their school doesn't play by the rules? In theory they tell the Appropriate Body but in practice who is going to complain about their assessor – the head and induction tutor – when these people can recommend a fail? The induction system assumes that all headteachers and LEAs know what they're doing and are reasonable people. Unfortunately, some NQTs wouldn't see it like that!

The headteacher has key responsibilities to (TTA, 2002a: 9):

1. ensure that each NQT in their school is provided with an appropriate induction programme, in line with national arrangements;
2. make a recommendation to the LEA, based on rigorous and fair assessment procedures, as to whether the NQT has met the induction standards;
3. designate an induction tutor (sometimes the head) for each NQT, and ensure that this person is adequately prepared and is able to work effectively in the role;
4. ensure that any duties assigned to you are reasonable;
5. ensure that you are provided with a timetable representing no more than 90 per cent of the average contact time normally allocated to more experienced teachers in the school, and ensure that the time released is protected, is distributed appropriately throughout the induction period and is used to support your professional development from the very outset of the induction period;
6. inform the LEA if you are at risk of failing to meet the induction standards and observe your teaching.

Unreasonable demands

Paragraph 26 of the induction circular says that teachers in their induction year should not be given a job description that makes unreasonable demands. Some NQTs have a job that contravenes almost all the guidance on what is considered appropriate or 'reasonable', such as in Figure 8.2.

NQTs should have a job that...	Peter's experience
Does not demand teaching outside the age range and subject(s) for which the NQT has been trained.	Compliance
Does not present the NQT on a day-to-day basis with acute or especially demanding discipline problems.	Discipline was a significant problem in the school. Peter had great problems controlling the pupils and very little help.
Involves regular teaching of the same class(es).	Yes, but Peter taught 16 different classes a week and did not get the reduced timetable until half way through the year.
Involves similar planning, teaching and assessment processes to those in which teachers working in substantive posts in the school are engaged.	Had no head of department for the spring and summer terms and little help from her in the autumn term. The only other teacher in the department was part-time, so the NQT had to support supply teachers.
Does not involve additional non-teaching responsibilities without the provision of appropriate preparation and support.	Peter was a form tutor, but had no support.

Figure 8.2   One NQT's job compared to what the induction circular lays down (Totterdell *et al*, 2002: 29)

What are 'reasonable' demands?

1. The post does not demand teaching outside the age range and subject(s) for which the NQT has been trained. Examples of contraventions of this include:
   - a maths teacher who has to teach PE without even the most basic of training in safety;
   - a history teacher who has to teach geography and RE to GCSE, even though he doesn't have such qualifications himself;
   - a KS1 and 2 trained teacher asked to teach reception.
2. The post does not present the NQT on a day-to-day basis with acute or especially demanding discipline problems. In an ideal world NQTs will be given timetables and classes that are comparatively easy. However, the easiest schools to work in often have the lowest staff turnover so NQTs are rarely employed in them. More typically, NQTs will find themselves working in a tough school where there are 'especially demanding discipline problems'. Often NQTs, because they are appointed after everyone else has put in their bid for their class or timetable, will end up with a rough deal even in comparison with experienced members of staff.

3. The post involves regular teaching of the same class or classes. This isn't usually an issue for NQTs but can be one for those who have entered a school as a supply or part-time teacher. During induction, you need to have a settled timetable, teaching the same pupils. If you are employed to work with pupils with special needs, or English as an additional language, you should not be expected to cover classes for absent colleagues or teach other pupils, unless by prior consent and for a good educational reason.

4. The post involves planning, teaching and assessment processes similar to those in which teachers working in substantive posts in the school are engaged. Realistically, this should be interpreted as not being expected to keep meticulous planning and assessment files like you did on teaching practice. Since, however, you are responsible for demonstrating that you meet the standards for the end of the induction period, you may need and want to keep more detailed paperwork than a colleague, who perhaps appears to do very little written planning – and yet gets by.

   One NQT had exactly the same number of Year 4 pupils as the parallel class teacher who had 20 years' experience. A new Year 4 girl arrived at the school. One would have thought that she would go into the experienced teacher's class but actually she joined the NQT's. The situation was made more difficult because the new girl couldn't read and hadn't been to school much before. This clearly made the NQT's planning, teaching and assessment harder than her colleague's.

5. The post does not involve additional non-teaching responsibilities without the provision of appropriate preparation and support. Additional non-teaching responsibilities can cover a range of things:
   – having a tutor group;
   – taking clubs at lunchtime or after school;
   – doing dinner duties;
   – having management responsibility.
   This clause is there to protect you – from yourself as much as from others. NQTs are typically terribly keen and enthusiastic and want to set up clubs, and innovate or make changes in the teaching of a curriculum area. However, all these things are

extremely demanding and can distract you from what should be your main focus – your everyday teaching. Once you have got that taped (if that ever happens!) you can develop further in other areas.

From the *TES forum*

'Since my HoD and mentor has been suspended from school I have been running a one-man show. I have been setting cover work, sorting out discipline problems for supply teachers and organising many things that are beyond my job description.'

If you find yourself taking an additional non-teaching responsibility you should have 'appropriate preparation and support'. This should start with an acknowledgement of the fact that you should not have to do this (refer to the induction circular) but will do so if given support. What would be helpful? Shadowing someone or sharing their tutor group, being given some training in the pastoral aspect of teaching or receiving help with managing parents would be valuable. If you find yourself a subject coordinator you should have a clear picture about what is expected of you, and training and time to do the role.

Induction tutors

The induction tutor has the day-to-day responsibility for your monitoring, support and assessment (TTA, 2001). They should be appropriately experienced and have regular contact with you. In many primary schools the induction tutor will be the deputy head or a phase coordinator. In a secondary school there are normally at least two levels of support – the head of department and a senior member of staff. Schools organise induction personnel in a range of ways, as Figure 8.3 shows. The terms by which roles are known varies.

One might imagine that the more people an NQT gets support from the better, and indeed we found instances where people benefited from getting help from a range of colleagues. However, some NQTs suffer as a result of responsibility being shared. For instance an

NQT in a secondary school with two levels of support suffered because the head of department did not do their job properly (observing every half-term, setting and reviewing targets and having regular meetings). It was only at the end of term that the induction coordinator realised this, however.

Primary school 1 (mono-support)	
Induction tutor:	Member of the senior management team.
Primary school 2 (mono-support)	
Induction tutor:	Headteacher.
Primary school 3 (bi-support)	
Induction tutor:	Member of the senior management team.
Mentor:	The parallel class teacher.
Primary school 4 (tri-support)	
Induction coordinator:	Member of the senior management team.
Induction tutor:	Year group leader.
Buddy mentor:	A recently qualified teacher.
Secondary school 1 (mono-support)	
Induction tutor:	Senior member of staff.
Secondary school 2 (bi-support)	
Induction coordinator:	Senior member of staff in charge of all NQTs in the school.
Induction tutor:	The head of department.
Secondary school 3 (tri-support)	
Induction coordinator:	Senior member of staff in charge of all NQTs in the school.
Induction tutor:	The head of department.
Buddy mentor:	A recently qualified teacher.
Secondary school 4 (tri-support)	
Induction tutor/coordinator:	A senior teacher who organises the induction programme, meetings, assessment reports, etc.
Academic mentor:	The head of department who advises on all subject-related matters.
Pastoral mentor:	A head of year who gives guidance on behaviour management and pastoral issues.
Secondary school 5 (multi-support)	
Staff development officer:	In charge of coordinating the induction programme for all NQTs and organises contracts, job descriptions, staff handbook and the pre-induction visits before the NQTs start work.
Subject mentor:	Head of the department that the NQT works in: supervises planning and teaching and gives subject specific input.
Pastoral mentor:	A head of year who gives guidance on behaviour management and pastoral issues.
Buddy mentor group:	A group of recently qualified teachers who provide a shoulder to cry on.

Figure 8.3   Organisation of induction personnel (Bubb *et al*, 2002: 29)

On the other hand, sharing responsibility means that the induction tutor's considerable workload is lessened. Shared responsibility has always worked best in schools with good communication systems (Earley and Kinder, 1994).

Responsibilities

Induction tutors are responsible for the following:

1. Making sure that you know and understand the roles and responsibilities of those involved in induction, including your own rights and your responsibility to take an active role in your professional development. Where NQTs are well supported, the induction tutor is up-to-date on induction requirements, has read the key documentation from the DfES and TTA, and is able to transmit this information to you and all others involved (Totterdell *et al*, 2002). Many schools now have an induction policy that gives clear guidance, particularly on everyone's rights and responsibilities.
2. Organising and implementing, in consultation with you, a tailored programme of monitoring, support and assessment that takes forward in a flexible way the action plan for your professional development and which takes into account the needs and strengths identified in the CEDP, the induction standards, and the specific context of the school.
3. Coordinating or carrying out observations of your teaching and organising follow up discussions. You should be observed at least once every half-term, and the first observation should take place within the first four weeks of your starting teaching. You should also have a post-observation discussion about your teaching. If different people are carrying out observations, they need to be coordinated so that you are not given conflicting messages.
4. Reviewing your progress against your objectives and the induction standards. Progress should be reviewed every half-term and summarised officially in the assessment forms at the end of each term. It's in everyone's interests therefore that objectives are SMART (specific, measurable, achievable, realistic and time-bound). I would also add that they should be clearly understandable, particularly in terms of the success criteria.

5. Making sure that you are fully informed about the nature and purpose of assessment in the induction period. One NQT who failed to complete his induction period satisfactorily complained that he did not always know when things were being said to him 'officially', that is, as part of the assessment process, and when people were offering advice supportively. It's essential that you are clear about the status of advice and comments, particularly since the monitoring, support and assessment may be carried out by the same person. It's difficult and uncomfortable for them as well as for you. Ask them playfully which hat they are wearing when they say certain things.

6. Ensuring that dated records are kept of monitoring, support, and formative and summative assessment activities undertaken, and their outcomes. There are examples of what these might look like in TTA materials, this book and my first book for induction tutors (Bubb, 2000).

The induction tutor needs to be fully aware of the requirements of the induction period and to have the skills, expertise and knowledge needed to work effectively in the role. This has been an issue for many NQTs. Too frequently, induction tutors have not been fully aware of what the induction period is all about. Many have been surprised that they are no longer simply mentors, there to help if the need arises. Their 'skills, knowledge and expertise' vary. Indeed, there is no definition of what is 'good enough' in this respect. Some have attended induction tutor training to help them in their role, but many have not. Some have read the key documentation and others have not. In particular, they should be able to provide or coordinate effective guidance and support, and to make rigorous and fair judgements about the new teacher's performance in relation to the induction standards. Quite a tall order!

If you have problems with your induction tutor or any other people who are responsible for your induction you must be proactive in trying to resolve them. It's you and the pupils you teach who will suffer. Here are some issues or problems relating to induction tutors that NQTs have encountered:

- hasn't time to do the job;
- doesn't want to do the job;

- not experienced in the NQT's subject or age group;
- doesn't know what to do;
- not planning how the induction release time should be spent – leaving it up to the NQT;
- not observing;
- observing too often;
- personality clash;
- different educational philosophy;
- NQT doesn't value what induction tutor has to say.

When one asks NQTs what they value most about their induction tutors they are very clear (Bubb, 2001: 23):

- They were always available for advice.
- They gave me a regular meeting time, even though they were busy.
- They were genuinely interested in how I was doing.
- They were honest and open, which encouraged trust.
- They listened to me – and didn't impose their own views.
- They made practical suggestions.
- They shared their expertise, ideas and resources.
- They were encouraging and optimistic – they made me feel good.
- They stopped me working myself into the ground by setting realistic objectives.
- They weren't perfect themselves, which was reassuring!
- They looked after me, keeping parents and the head off my back.
- Their feedback after observations was useful. Good to get some praise and ideas for improvements.
- It helped when they wrote the end of term reports because these gave us a clear picture of how we were doing.
- They were well organised, and if they said they'd do something they did it.

More than anything, NQTs value someone who gives them time. This is a very precious resource in schools. Induction tutors often have many other time-consuming roles and their time spent on induction is rarely funded. The DfES has rightly devoted money to ensuring that NQTs have a 10 per cent reduced timetable, but there is little extra to cover the potentially enormous costs of paying the people who are doing the support, monitoring and assessment. As ever, much has to be done on goodwill.

> ### From the *TES forum*
>
> 'My induction tutor was wondering if there was a certain amount of time that induction tutors should get for completion of NQT things, such as filling in forms, etc or are they just supposed to do everything after school and in their own time? I don't actually think that my induction tutor was actually told about the kinds of things she would be expected to do by the head. She thought it was more of a supportive role and a friendly shoulder to cry on!'

There isn't any allocated time for induction tutors to do their job. This is a big problem, particularly as many people are like your induction tutor: they take on the role thinking that it's just a supportive one whereas actually it takes up a lot of time and calls for a great deal of skill. In our research for the DfES (Totterdell *et al*, 2002) we said that there should be earmarked funding for the induction tutors. The end of term report takes about two hours to write; meetings take at least 30 minutes a week; observations take half a day every half-term if you count the preparation and feedback too. So the job significantly adds to workload. Headteachers need to realise this and reduce induction tutors' teaching load accordingly.

nine

Making the most of induction

- The CEDP and setting objectives
- The individualised induction programme
- How to spend your reduced timetable
- Observing others
- Being observed
- Reviewing progress
- Being assessed
- Problems with assessment

Induction exists to help new teachers. Don't see it as a threat, a barrier to get across, but view it as a great opportunity to be helped to make a great deal of progress in a short amount of time. The Career Entry and Development Profile (CEDP) (TTA, 2003b) should act as a guide from training into induction. It also has useful supplementary guidance and pro formas.

The CEDP and setting objectives

The CEDP asks you some useful questions to help you reflect on what you need to work on in the short and longer term – and why. Take time to go through this process thoughtfully with your induction tutor, perhaps after the first week. You should be setting objectives for what you want to do better – and to get you where you want to go. Your main concern is to be a good class teacher and meet the induction standards. But you may have a further ambition that you want to work towards. Setting yourself a goal, a target, an objective (don't get bogged down in the semantics) will provide you with a framework for doing a complex job at a very fast pace. Objectives encourage you to prioritise and give you a sense of achievement when they are met.

Don't stick slavishly to what you wrote in your CEDP at the end of your training course or at the start of induction. The chances are that your new job makes much of this irrelevant. You might have been very good at managing behaviour on teaching practice but now have the class from hell. Think about what's going to really help you now – and what will make you a better teacher of your pupils. Your induction tutor will help you prioritise and pace yourself. It's good to look at and perhaps revise your objectives after an observation of your teaching. Remember that your aim is to meet the induction standards and help your pupils learn.

Some NQTs have plenty of discussion about what they need to improve but no specific objectives. This is a missed opportunity. The very act of writing objectives down clarifies what you need to do, and helps ensure they're SMART – specific, measurable, achievable, relevant and time-bound. Ask yourself if the objective is SMART and adapt it accordingly. An objective like 'Improve control' is too large, and could be a lifetime's work. It's better to be more specific about what needs most urgent attention, such as: 'By the end of term improve control particularly after break times, during independent activities and when tidying up.' This is achievable and relevant to your class teaching.

Action plan

When you're happy with the objective, break it down into bite-sized chunks – steps or success criteria – and think what you'll have to do and what help you'll need. Write this action plan in the easiest way. The CEDP has some formats but Figure 9.1 is a useful format for a working document.

Aim for an objective to be met within a half-term, when reviews with your induction tutor take place. This will encourage you to be realistic, focussed and give you a well-deserved sense of achievement.

Name: Lucy	Date: 1 November		Date objective to be met: 16 December
Objective: To improve control, particularly after playtimes, in independent literacy activities, at tidying-up time, and home time.			

Success criteria	Actions	When	Progress
Gets attention more quickly	Brainstorm attention-getting devices. Use triangle, etc to get attention.	4.11	7.11 Triangle made children more noisy – try cymbal
Rarely shouts	Voice management course. Project the voice. Don't talk over children.	19.11	23.11 Using more range in voice – working!
Plans for behaviour management	Glean ideas from other teachers through discussion and observation. Watch videos on behaviour management strategies. Write notes for behaviour management on plans.	4.11	12.11 Improvement through lots of tips, staying calm and being more positive Not perfect and exhausting but better
Successful procedures for sorting out disputes after playtimes	Glean ideas from other teachers. Ask playground supervisors to note serious incidents. Children to post messages in incident box.	11.11	18.11 Incident box really working for those who can write and I can now tell when there's a serious problem
Successful procedures for tidying	Discuss what other teachers do. Start tidying earlier and time it with reward for beating record. Sanctions for the lazy.	18.11	25.11 Sand timer for tidying working well though still a few children not helping Might try minutes off playtime
Successful procedures for home time	Discuss ideas with other teachers. Monitors to organise things to take home. Start home time procedures earlier and time them (with rewards?).	25.11	2.12 Changed routine so tidy earlier Some Y6 children helping give out things to take home
Children succeed in independent literacy activities	Ideas from literacy coordinator. Change seating for groups. Differentiate work. Discuss with additional adults.	2.12	9.12 All class doing same independent activity working better Mrs H helping
Review			

Figure 9.1   An action plan to meet an objective (Bubb *et al*, 2002: 111)

The individualised induction programme

The vast majority of NQTs feel under tremendous pressure in their first year of teaching. In a way, this has increased with the advent of statutory induction, particularly the formal assessment aspect of it. The individualised induction programme, however, is the key to your successful progress, and sanity. You have release time and rights that previous cohorts of NQTs have not had. You need to make the most of them – you'll never have the opportunity again.

Planning an effective programme, however, isn't easy. There are many components, as we shall see. There is no such thing as a perfect model because every context and every NQT is different. Even in the same school, what works for one person may not work for another. The statutory guidance emphasises that induction programmes should be 'tailored to individual needs'. Your induction tutor is responsible for drawing up the programme, but you need to play a big part to ensure it meets your needs.

A significant feature of the statutory induction programmes is that they should involve 'a combination of support, monitoring and assessment'. In the past, support has been the focus of most programmes. Monitoring and assessment have been very much in the background. There should be a balance between support, monitoring and assessment, and you should alert people if you feel that one is dominating to the detriment of others.

The induction programme should have specific weekly events, involving support, monitoring and assessment. The filling in of a diary sheet such as Figure 9.2 will help you plan and briefly record specifics, with your induction tutor. It can be used for evaluating the programme, and as a record to show the LEA and other external monitors. It shows how all the elements can be brought together in a manageable way, and how the programme can respond to the NQT's stages of development and half-termly objectives through the year. The school-based programme has several elements that need to be seen as a whole in contributing to your development:

- school/phase/departmental staff meetings and CPD;
- meetings with the induction tutor;
- how to spend your reduced timetable;
- observation of your teaching.

Oliver's autumn first half-term induction programme

Objectives:
To organise the classroom to ensure effective learning
To improve behaviour management
To gain confidence in relating to parents

Observation of NQT	NQT release time for induction	Induction tutor meetings	Staff, department meetings and INSET
6 September	10 September LEA induction programme – the standards relating to parents	The Career Entry Development Profile	Key Stage 3 strategy training
13 September	Organise room Label resources	Classroom organisation	
20 September Observation focussing on organisation and control	Observe Y7 focussing on organisation and behaviour management	Feedback and discussion following observation	Planning
27 September	29 September LEA induction programme – classroom management Written reflection	Behaviour management	Parents' evening arrangements
4 October	Prepare for parents' evening Display	Parents' evening tips	Numeracy assessment
11 October	Observe own Y8 class being taught by supply teacher Written reflection	Monitor planning	Review behaviour policy
18 October	Observe Y9 Written reflection	Review of the half-term objectives Set new objectives	Review behaviour policy

Figure 9.2   An induction programme

School staff meetings and INSET

School staff meetings and CPD (Continuing Professional Development) will have an impact on your progress and so should be noted on your induction programme.

Meetings with the induction tutor

There should be regular planned meetings with the induction tutor. These should happen throughout the year. It's very easy to let them slide because of other demands on time, but you really will benefit from attention, particularly because of the formal assessment at the end of each term. Often, successful NQTs are left to their own devices, but they too need to be challenged in order to become even better teachers. One said 'I think I was neglected because everyone was happy with me. But now I feel disappointed in myself because I know I should be doing better than I am.'

How often should induction meetings take place?

The answer to this question will depend on how much support you are getting from others. For instance, year group planning and assessment meetings will be of enormous benefit. Similarly, making friends with someone on the staff with whom you can discuss issues will ease the burden on the induction tutor – as long as advice from different quarters isn't contradictory. NQTs and schools will also have views on the amount of support they think NQTs need. Generally, I would recommend weekly meetings at first, maybe reducing to fortnightly after the first term. The TTA framework (2002a: 6), however, implies a minimum of a meeting at the beginning and end of each half-term.

How long should meetings last?

Meetings should consist of quality time. Chats in the staffroom at playtime may be pleasant but cannot take the place of planned meetings. A regular meeting slot of about half an hour will be seen as the appropriate time to raise matters. Quality time induction meetings should have:

- no interruptions;
- a venue with minimal disturbance from phone calls, pupils, other teachers, etc;
- a fixed start and finish time;
- an agreed agenda, albeit informal and flexible;
- an agreed aim, probably linked to the induction standards;
- a focus on the NQT, rather than the induction tutor's anecdotes;
- a record of any agreed outcomes.

How to spend your reduced timetable

How are you spending this release time? Any teacher will tell you it's a very precious resource, so make the most of it. It's all too easy to spend your induction time doing things that are immediately necessary – marking, say, or displays – but it's not always a good use of time in the long run. There are many different ways to spend induction release time (Bubb, 2001: 86):

- reflecting on progress so far;
- attending induction and other courses;
- observing other teachers in the school;
- observing teachers in other schools;
- observing someone teach your class(es);
- observing someone teach a lesson that you have planned;
- observing how pupils of different ages learn;
- looking at resources in the school, such as computer programs;
- visiting local education centres, museums and venues for outings;
- arranging a school outing;
- looking at the educational possibilities of the local environment;
- working with the SENCO on writing individual education plans (IEPs);
- reading pupils' previous records and reports;
- making some in-depth assessments of individual pupils;
- improving subject knowledge through reading, observation, discussion;

- analysing planning systems in order to improve their own;
- analysing marking and record-keeping systems in order to improve own;
- standardisation meetings;
- writing reports;
- planning a lesson based on the thorough assessment of pieces of work;
- making resources and displaying work;
- learning more about strategies for teaching the pupils with special needs;
- learning more about strategies for teaching pupils with EAL;
- learning more about strategies for teaching very able pupils;
- meeting with parents and preparing for parents' evenings;
- meeting with outside agencies (social workers, educational psychologists);
- updating the professional portfolio and completing documentation;
- discussing lesson observations;
- meeting with the induction tutor and other staff.

When considering what to do, ask yourself whether it will help you meet the standards for the end of the induction year and whether you are going to be a better teacher as a result. If you make specific plans, you're less likely to lose your release time. Link activities to the objectives you're setting with your induction tutor. If marking takes hours, set yourself an objective to improve it. Spend some time reading articles on the subject and getting other people's tips for how they do it more quickly than you. Looking at their systems and what they write is really useful.

Spend time with other staff, like the special needs coordinator (SENCO) or the gifted and talented coordinator. Find out how best to teach certain groups of children. Talk through specific problems with them as well as with your induction tutor. If you're in the secondary sector, it's fascinating to track a pupil for half a day and see what their experience of school is. You learn lots from seeing the styles of different subject teachers, and you gain an insight into how students learn. Certainly, helping pupils to make connections between subjects can really help to improve their work.

Making resources, reading books and articles, and finding ways to make your assessment systems more effective are all useful ways to spend time. Look through resources in the school – hunt around and you could find something fantastic by accident!

An important decision that needs to be made early on is whether you should join a programme with other NQTs. Local education authorities, colleges and educational consultants often run these courses. The big advantage of joining such a programme is that you gain a great deal from talking to other NQTs. You'll feel enormously comforted by hearing that others are going through the same problems. No matter how sympathetic experienced members of staff are, the solitary NQT in a school often feels that they are the only one who cannot, for instance, get their class to assembly on time. Enrolment on an externally organised programme also eases the burden on schools to provide training. However, it can only supplement the individualised school programme, not replace it. Check that they're covering what you need to improve. Don't just look at ones run locally – cast your net wider to find just the right one. Remember that you're being inducted into the profession, not just your school. Keep your ears open to everything, but keep thinking about how you could use ideas in your classroom.

You may benefit from finding out more about outside agencies, particularly if they see any of your pupils. You could sit in on some of the work of educational psychologists, health visitors, educational welfare officers, speech therapists or occupational therapists. Go to different sorts of educational settings. If your school has a link with a special school or pupil referral unit, make an appointment to visit it and look around. Get to know the local area around the school, looking at where the children live and the places they talk about. Some could have educational possibilities but, even if they don't, the experience will give you some insight into the children's lives and help you keep up with break-time conversations.

It's a good idea to plan a class visit, while you have the safety net of still being a new teacher. It takes lots of organisation and even choosing a good venue can take ages. You need to visit it beforehand, and do a risk assessment of all points on the journey and at the venue. This will give you the chance to think through potential problems and avoid things that could go wrong.

Reflection time is a must. It should have higher status and time allocated to it. Analyse why things go well, and why other things don't go so well. Most of all, make sure you spend the time becoming a better teacher.

Another problem with the release time is what happens to your class when you are not there. Some NQTs preferred not to take their 10 per cent release time because of the disruption to the class caused by different supply teachers. They found that they would have to teach lessons again because the pupils had not learned things with the supply teacher. This is a particular problem for new teachers in Scotland, with 0.3 of their job being covered by a relief teacher.

From the TES forum

'My relief does her own marking and preparation, but my friend has to do all the planning, all the photocopying and preparation, for the relief to just waltz in at 8.55 to ask "what am I doing today?"'

In almost all the schools I've had contact with, there were difficulties with cover for the 10 per cent release time. A comment made at one school was 'It's very important to have school staff covering the induction release time. Classes go haywire when they have a supply teacher.' One primary school, which had four NQTs, employed a further NQT so that an experienced member of staff could be non-class-based and so cover all the NQTs' release time.

Observing others

An excellent way of spending your release time is to observe others at work. You'll find out so much about teaching and learning. Over the year, observe a range of teachers and other staff, age groups, specialist groups, subjects and lessons at different times of the day. Observe in other schools, too. Keep a record of observations on a format such as Figure 9.3.

Observing a lesson so that you get something out of it is not easy, as I said in Chapter 3. Try to observe a range of teachers and assistants, age groups, subjects and lessons at different times of the day. Observe in schools with and without beacon status, too. It's very cheering to see that everyone has similar problems and fascinating to study the

Date	Time	Class	Teacher and school	Subject and focus

Figure 9.3   Record of observations of other teachers by NQT

different ways people manage them. Don't always observe experienced and successful teachers. You'll learn a great deal from seeing other trainees, NQTs and supply teachers. If you watch a class you've taught being led by someone else you can see the children's learning, behaviour and reactions, and how another teacher handles them.

You need to have a focus for your observation. There is so much to see that you can end up getting overwhelmed. First, decide what you want to observe. Ideally, link the observation to one of your objectives – something that you want to develop. For instance, if you want to improve pace in introductions, arrange to observe that. Notice the speed of the exposition, how many pupils answer questions and how the teacher manages to move them on, how instructions are given, resources distributed, and how off-task behaviour is dealt with. Here are some examples of how some NQTs chose what to observe:

Some NQT observations

Julian was interested in developing his explanations of mathematical concepts so that he could make things clearer and not get thrown by pupils' questions. With this clearly in mind, he chose to observe maths lessons where new topics were being started. He learned the benefits of rock-solid subject knowledge and scaffolding information. He also gained a broader repertoire of questioning techniques that he was able to try out in his own teaching.

Diana had problems with behaviour management, so observed a teacher with a good reputation for control. She gained some ideas, but found that much of this experienced teacher's control was 'invisible' – he just cleared his throat and the class became quiet. So, she observed a supply teacher, and someone with only a little more experience than herself. It was hard to persuade them to let her observe, but when they realised how fruitful the experience and the discussions afterwards would be, they accepted. These lessons, though not so perfectly controlled, gave Diana much more to think about and she learned lots of useful strategies. Both teachers found it useful to have Diana's views on the lesson, as a non-threatening observer, so they too gained from the experience.

Miranda's objective was to share learning intentions with pupils so she observed a teacher who was known to be good at this. She not only listened well to the teacher's explanation of what he wanted the pupils to achieve but saw that he wrote different lesson outcomes for each group under the headings 'What I'm Looking For'. As well as focussing on the teacher, she watched the pupils carefully and spoke to them about their understanding of what they were doing and why. This gave her insight into children's learning and areas of confusion.

Once you've decided what you would like to observe you need to arrange it. It's useful for your induction tutor to be involved in the arrangements, particularly for observations in another school. Their involvement will lend weight to your request and increase the chances of it happening. You need to discuss the observation with the teacher. Remember that they are doing you a favour and that they'll probably be apprehensive about you being in the classroom so you will need to be sensitive. Be clear about what you would like to see, and why. You will need to arrange a mutually convenient time. This isn't always easy because of timetabling constraints.

When you're observing

If possible, read the lesson plan, paying particular attention to the learning objective. Is it a useful objective, and is it shared with the pupils? Choose somewhere to sit that is outside the direct line of the teacher's vision, but where you can see the pupils and what the teacher is doing. When the pupils are doing activities, move around to ascertain the effectiveness of the explanation, organisation and choice of task. Look at different groups (girls and boys; high, average and low attainers; and pupils with English as an additional language) to see whether everyone's needs are being met.

Think about the pupils' learning and what it's about the teaching that is helping or hindering it. Try to note cause and effect. For instance, what was it about the teacher's delivery that caused pupils' rapt attention, or fidgeting? Note what pupils actually achieve. Teachers are not always aware that some pupils have only managed to write the date and that others have exceeded expectations. Look through pupils' books to get a feel of what they have achieved. Avoid teaching the pupils yourself or interfering in any way. This is very tempting! Pupils will often expect you to help them with spellings, for instance, but once you help one others will ask. This will distract you from your central purpose, which is to observe. Look friendly and positive throughout, even (and especially) if things aren't going well. Being observed is nerve-racking no matter how experienced the teacher is.

Think about the teaching and learning you have seen, and try to talk about it with the teacher. Note down a few key things you have seen, using Figure 9.4 or Figures 3.1 or 3.2 in Chapter 3. Is there anything that could impact on your teaching? It's even worthwhile observing teaching that you do not like because it makes you think about your own practice, and almost forces you to articulate your educational philosophy – something we do too little of.

Observing other teachers – what have you learned? What could you implement in your classroom?	
Teacher:　　　　　　Year group:　　　　　Date and time:	
Arrangement of the room	What and when implemented
Resources	
Behaviour management	
Teaching strategies	

Figure 9.4　Format for recording ideas from observations

Being observed

You'll be observed at least once every half-term when you're an NQT, and often more. In our research for the DfES (Totterdell *et al*, 2002) I was surprised to find that 89 per cent of NQTs found being observed really useful. I had thought that people would have been sick of being observed during their training, and see more observations as an unnecessary stress. The views of this NQT were typical:'It's vital. It's just so informative having someone watch you teach because you can't see everything and sometimes you don't see what you do well, just the things you need to develop.'

Another considered it 'the most nerve-racking part but I think it's the most effective'. Many spoke of it as a positive and constructive experience. One NQT loved being observed: 'I love showing my kids off as well… I choose my lowest sets… It raises their self-esteem and it makes me feel really proud of them' (Bubb *et al*, 2002: 139).

However, not all schools are as organised about carrying out observations as they should be. Over a quarter of NQTs weren't observed every half-term, nor during their first four weeks. The reasons for this were:

- There were too many other things to do at the beginning of the school year.
- Induction tutors thought that NQTs needed time to settle before being observed. This was often misplaced kindness.
- Induction tutors didn't know that they should do an early observation and hadn't been trained to do so.

Be proactive in asking for the date of forthcoming observations. Some NQTs have had observations on the last day of term with no notice. A variety of people observe NQTs teach: induction tutors, headteachers, mentors, heads of department, and representatives from the Appropriate Bodies. Some NQTs in our research found feedback from induction tutors more useful than from people outside the school. Others valued and were motivated by feedback from people they considered experts. LEA advisers or inspectors observed one-third of NQTs. For one NQT this was such a valuable experience that she described it as a turning point: 'He boosted my confidence immensely.'

Try to see observation of your teaching as an opportunity to get some really useful feedback – and not as a threat. Observation is a powerful tool for assessing and monitoring your progress. Used well, it can be a way to support you, because observation gives such a detailed picture and enables very specific objectives to be set. The value of observation, however, depends on how well it's planned, executed and discussed afterwards. It's almost always a stressful experience.

The people observing you may also find observing stressful, perhaps because they feel inexperienced and uncertain of the best way to go about it. The year group or area of the curriculum may not be familiar. They may feel that the quality of their observation and feedback will compare unfavourably to that of others. They will also be mindful of the responsibility to help you make progress, while maintaining a good relationship. This can lead some observers to be too kind and others to be too harsh. Trainees sometimes feel that they are not being sufficiently challenged. This is particularly true if you are very successful, but you too need to be helped to develop professionally. You can help this process by being very open to ideas, and accepting and even encouraging constructive criticism.

Before an observation

Make sure you know what notice you'll have of an observation, when you're going to be observed, for how long, and by whom. Discuss nitty gritty things such as exactly when they'll arrive and leave, where they will sit, how their presence is to be explained to the pupils and how they should be introduced. Find out in what format the observer is going to write (see Figure 9.5) and when you'll be able to get feedback on the lesson.

It's useful to have a focus for the observation – something that is being looked at in particular. This won't stop the observer from noticing and commenting on other things but will ensure that you have information on the key area that you are working on. Think about what will really help you. Here are examples of what some people chose as a focus:

- Feedback (oral and written):
  - How well do different groups know what they are doing?
  - How well do different groups know why they are doing it?

- How do different groups know how well they have done?
- What sort of feedback does the teacher use, and to which children?

● Learning objectives:
- How well are these conveyed?
- Are they appropriate for different groups of children?
- Do the activities enable them to achieve the objectives?
- Do all children meet them well enough?

● Management:
- Is there good control at different parts of the lesson and of all the children?
- How is off-task behaviour managed?

Summary of classroom observation
Strengths of the lesson Well done, Miranda, this was a lesson that I enjoyed. You have so many talents as a teacher! In particular the strengths of this lesson were: • Strong voice, good intonation – clear explanations. • Warmth towards the students – your smile, eye contact, facial expressions and body language all work to encourage and give students the confidence to take risks. V positive feedback and use of praise to boost self confidence. • Good questioning especially stretching EAL pupils to explain what they mean. • Excellent control – all the above contribute help in this area but you are also very confident yourself and this helps. You expect them to behave in a certain way, and they do. You handle the odd misbehaviour briskly with a change of tone ('Don't call out, Michael') and good use of body language (turning away, not giving attention) but then you catch M being good – brilliant! • Well resourced and organised. • Clear plan, with timings. • Good use made of the OHP. • Good use of support teacher at start of lesson and in reading out a paragraph to emphasise the tense difference. • Good choice of text that motivates and is part of their culture.
Areas for further development Try to increase the learning of more of the students more of the time, eg: • Share learning objectives – WALT & WILF? • Big picture of the lesson. • More paired work: discussing whose autobiography they'd like to read, writing and maybe ordering chapter headings. • Having a plenary for them and you to evaluate learning and progress. • Make even more use of support teacher.
Objectives Plan lessons to increase the learning of more of the students more of the time.
Teacher's comment:
Signatures:

Figure 9.5 Summary of classroom observation

- Is there a brisk pace that keeps children's attention?
- Are resources appropriate, organised and distributed to make best use of time?

Chapter 3 has some ideas for how to prepare for an observation. Here is a summary:

- Be completely prepared.
- Plan with even more care.
- Have a copy of the lesson plan for the observer.
- Be absolutely clear about what you want the pupils to learn and do.
- Make sure your teaching and the activities match the objectives.
- Think through every stage of the lesson to pre-empt problems.
- Have as much stuff written on the board beforehand.
- Think about what the person observing you is looking for.
- Address things that haven't gone well before.
- Look at the QTS standards again.
- Show that you're making progress against your current objectives.
- Plan to please – observers have their own pet loves and hates.
- Get a good night's sleep.
- Do everything you can to feel confident – wear your favourite teaching clothes, encourage other people to boost you up.
- Tell yourself that you're going to teach well, and believe it.

Being nervous when observed is perfectly normal, and most people can tell when you are and make allowances for this. One way of coping with nerves is to understand why you get worried: then you can do something about it. Common concerns and possible solutions are listed in Figure 3.3 in Chapter 3.

During the observation

Give the observer a copy of your plan, so that they are clear why you are doing certain things, but otherwise just block out the observer and focus on teaching and learning. Think of your teaching as a performance, and go for gold. Try to keep to time, but be flexible where necessary. Don't forget to have a plenary to reinforce and assess learning. Try to demonstrate the standards. Don't feel inhibited by the presence of the observer – try to be natural.

Don't panic if things start to go wrong. Think on your feet. Most NQTs have some lessons that go swimmingly, others that are okay and occasional disasters. There are a huge number of factors to do with you and what you're teaching and then a whole heap to do with different classes, what lesson they've just had, and what time of day it is.

The post-observation discussion

Here is a tip in response to a posting to the New Teacher Forum Web site:

Top tip!

Q: 'My first observation was just before half-term. Feedback – 11 days later – was "everything fine". But I was disappointed by the delays and the superficiality.'

A: You are right to object. Your induction tutor may have thought she was doing you a favour, so tell her how you feel. You should be observed at least once in every six to eight weeks. The first one should have been within the first four weeks, not just before half-term. It would be wise to keep a record of your induction support and assessment, and note issues such as the late first observation. At future planning stages, discuss arrangements such as dates, times and the focus of the observation. Ensure that your induction tutor knows what you would find most useful. Arrange a time to discuss the lesson, and a length of time, ideally within 24 hours of the observation.

The value of the dialogue that takes place when feedback is given after a lesson observation cannot be over-emphasised. Its effect, however, depends on both the quality of the feedback and the relationship of trust between you and the observer. Reflecting on your own teaching through discussing a lesson observation may be your most valuable learning experience.

After the lesson, think about what the pupils learned and why, so that you're ready to answer the inevitable 'How do you think it went?' question. Before discussing the lesson, reflect on it yourself. What were you pleased with? What could have gone better? How did your teaching affect the progress pupils made? Don't be disheartened if the lesson didn't go well. See it as an event to be learnt from and given advice on. It was a one-off performance, a snapshot, and things can be different tomorrow.

Use the feedback to discuss the minutiae of the lesson, and to get ideas for improvements. There's no such thing as a perfect teacher (except in your mind) so your lesson doesn't have to be perfect. You need to show that you're reflective, making progress and acting on advice. However, if you think your teaching is criticised unfairly, make sure you explain the reasoning behind your actions. Stick up for yourself. Ask for clarification of anything you're unsure of. Try to summarise the main points of the discussion, asking the observer if they agree. Ask for advice and ideas. Afterwards, reflect on the discussion. Feel good about the positive comments and think about how to improve.

Reviewing progress

Professional review meeting
Date and time:
Agenda
Things that are going well
Things to improve
Progress on current objectives
Date of next meeting:
Signatures:

Figure 9.6 Professional review meeting

Your progress should be reviewed half-termly using a pro forma such as Figure 9.6. Take stock and appreciate what you've learned and how far you've come on your journey to being the best teacher in the world. Maybe you've had to go off course from the way you want to teach for all manner of pragmatic reasons – say, the kids behave better in rows but that's not how you want to work in the long term. Look at your induction entitlement. Did you get it all last term? If not, you need to make sure it happens in the future. Alternatively, people may have provided good support in the first term, but then forget that you're still an NQT (you're so good!) and need help throughout the year.

Be clear about what support you want. Have you got a clear picture of how well you're doing? The end of term assessment report should have detailed this. If the head and induction tutor have decided that you're not making satisfactory progress you should get extra support and monitoring from the school and LEA to enable you to pass the induction standards by the end of the year. Most of you will be making satisfactory or better progress. You'll always be thinking about what's going to help you be a better class teacher. Don't get distracted from this most complex and important journey. Running clubs and taking other roles in the school can be an unnecessary and lengthy diversion.

Make sure that your programme, like Julian's (see Figure 9.7), is individualised, is focussed on what you need to get better at and has the right balance of support, monitoring and assessment. His objective is clear, and broken down into bite-sized activities and specific support because he's thought about what he needs to improve and what help he'll need. He's arranged help not only from the induction tutor but the assessment coordinator.

Being assessed

Many NQTs worry about what they must do to pass induction. Don't panic. If you've been teaching for a year you will have been doing all that is necessary to meet the standards. Get them out and assess yourself against them. You will have been setting targets, planning, teaching, assessing, managing pupils, using individual education plans, working with support staff, talking to parents, implementing school policies and taking an active part in your

Julian's induction programme – 1st half of spring term **Objective: to improve procedures for assessment to inform planning**			
Observed on	Things to do in 10% reduced timetable	Induction tutor meeting focus	School INSET
6 January	Review last term's progress	Plan half-term meetings and activities	Thinking skills
13 January	Get a detailed picture of what three pupils can do	Assessment coordinator – target setting	Thinking skills
20 January	23 January course on assessment	24 January induction tutor training	Target setting
27 January	Set targets	Assessment coordinator – monitoring targets	Charity week
3 February Observation focussing on assessment	Look at marking and record keeping of two other teachers	Discuss observation	Numeracy
10 February	Observation focussing on assessment in lesson	Review progress	Parents' evening

Figure 9.7   An example of an induction programme

professional development. You don't need to collect any evidence for the standards other than what you do as part of your job, and what others have written about you. However, look through the standards to check you haven't left any gaps.

Some schools expect NQTs to keep teaching practice-level folders of evidence (Bubb *et al*, 2002), but this is unnecessary. You keep enough paperwork as a class teacher. Don't worry about standards that don't apply to you – if you don't teach pupils with special needs, you can't contribute to individual education plans.

The three formal assessment meetings are very important, and valuable, in reviewing progress. They should be held towards the end of each term, and are the forums for the termly assessment reports to be discussed and written. Schools are obviously busy at the end of term, so put a date in the diary for your assessment meetings with the head and induction tutor. Choose a date that is convenient to all and make sure that at least a week's notice is given. It is ideal if it takes place during the school day, though in practice many schools find this hard to organise. Think carefully about a realistic start and finish time – it will be important to feel fresh. The length of the meeting will depend on the degree of agreement about your performance and how much preparatory work on the report has been done. A straightforward case for which all are well briefed should take not much more than half an hour. Holding the meeting in your classroom may give you a feeling of control that may not be present in the headteacher's office. It also means that there is easy access to further evidence, such as pupils' work.

Standardised three-page forms have to be filled in and sent to the Appropriate Body within 10 days of the meeting. Appropriate Bodies will usually set their own deadlines for reports. The form for the first and second terms requires the headteacher to tick one of two statements, either: 1) The above named teacher's progress indicates that he/she will be able to meet the requirements for the satisfactory completion of the induction period; or 2) The above named teacher is not making satisfactory progress towards the requirements for the satisfactory completion of the induction period.

You'll know if you're at risk of failure because observations of your teaching and the first and/or second term's reports would have said your progress was unsatisfactory. If they did not, you are unlikely to be anywhere near failing. The system does not allow for last-minute shocks. To be sure, check with your head. If you aren't making satisfactory progress after the first or second term, the assessment report and meeting should mean that you're clear about what you have to do to improve.

The headteacher must tick the kinds of monitoring and support that have been in place during the term. The induction tutor will probably be responsible for writing the reports. Make sure you are happy with what is written about you – that it is a fair reflection of you. During the assessment meeting, suggest additions or revisions to the wording of the assessment form.

NQTs can choose whether or not to make a comment on the report, and are given a box in which to write. I think you should write something since the whole emphasis in induction is on NQTs being proactive and reflective. Some NQTs say which parts of their induction programme have been most useful; others defend themselves; others write about what they feel are their strengths and areas for development.

Your head has to say whether or not you're meeting the induction and QTS standards at the end of your third term. This becomes a recommendation that is sent to the LEA as the Appropriate Body. The LEA should visit schools that have NQTs to ensure the standards are uniform, and be involved with new teachers whose term one and two assessment reports indicated problems. The local authority makes the final decision as to who passes, and will send a list of those who have passed to the General Teaching Council. Those who fail are deregistered from the GTC and never again allowed to teach in a maintained school or non-maintained special school. Don't worry, only one in 500 have failed.

Those at risk of failing are often encouraged by schools and the LEA to leave before they complete their third term. They can complete their last term on induction at another school and at another time. Often this fresh start can pay dividends, and it's the route I'd take if I were failing.

Ensure that observations of your teaching in the last term show you at your best. Really go for it and learn from the feedback. From now on, you'll only definitely be observed just once a year for performance management, so make the most of someone's insight into your work.

Sign the report, make a comment, take a photocopy and check (and keep checking) that it is received by the Appropriate Body to ensure that, in the words of television's Blackadder, you're 'not at home to Mr Cock-up'.

Case study: how Jo completed the assessment on William (Bubb *et al,* 2002: 171)

Both Jo and William evaluated how they thought he was meeting the standards by jotting notes about each. They discussed their views, ensuring that evidence existed for all assertions. She drafted sections of the report against the three headings of the standards aiming for a word length of 300 words. She wrote an overall message in the first section and then elaborated. Where space allowed, she referred briefly to evidence.

Jo gave a copy to the headteacher and William to look at just before the meeting. At the meeting all discussed what was written and suggested changes. The revised agreed document was then given to William for a written comment, and then he, Jo and the headteacher signed it. All were given copies and the original was sent to the LEA.

The final assessment report

The last report doesn't require any writing, if you have met the induction standards, but you should discuss how well you're meeting the standards. Use the time to get a clear picture of your strengths and successes, and celebrate them. Discuss what you should develop in your second year when you get slotted into the school's performance management arrangements.

In cases of either a successful or a failing NQT, the headteacher is only making a recommendation to the Appropriate Body (usually the LEA). It is up to them to make the final decision. In the case of failures, many LEAs will want to observe the NQT, but this is not statutory. The LEA is responsible for making sure that the assessment of the NQT was accurate and reliable, that the NQT's objectives were set appropriately and that they were supported. LEAs can grant extensions to the induction period but only in exceptional circumstances. These are where, for reasons unforeseen and/or beyond the control of one or more of the parties involved, it is unreasonable to expect the NQT to meet the requirements by the end of the induction period or there is insufficient evidence on which a decision can be made about whether the induction requirements have been met (DfEE, 2000: paragraph 15).

NQTs can appeal to the General Teaching Council (GTC) against the Appropriate Body's decision to extend the induction period or fail them.

The assessment procedure in Scotland

NQTs in Wales have to meet the standard, which is in Appendix 2, and procedures are similar to those in England. The system of assessing new teachers in Scotland is different. In their first year, new teachers, or 'probationers' as they are called, are given 'provisional registration'. By the end of the year they have to demonstrate that they meet the 'Standard for Full Registration' (this is in Appendix 3). As in England, the school is responsible for the recommendation, although the Scottish General Teaching Council awards full registration. The school has to make one of the following recommendations:

- that full registration be granted; or
- that the period of provisional registration be extended; or
- that registration be withdrawn.

Do you notice that the school has the option of recommending an extension? This can't happen in England. In Scotland the profile (the assessment form) is completed twice, rather than three times as in England. It is eight pages long and combines the interim and final profile:

Page 1 indicates personal details about the teacher.
Page 2 provides a list of meetings held with the support.
Page 3 provides information relating to the observed teaching sessions.
Pages 4 and 5 indicate the range of professional development opportunities that the teacher has undertaken.
Page 6 provides a statement of the Standard for Full Registration.
Page 7 provides an opportunity for comments to be made in relation to the probationer teacher's strengths in terms of various elements of the standard.
Page 8 on the interim profile indicates agreed targets and action; on the final profile it indicates the agreed targets and action and provides an opportunity for the teacher to comment on his/her proposed plans for the subsequent five years.

Problems with assessment

Well, that's what is meant to happen and for many people the process is straightforward and reassuring. Unfortunately there are cases of poor practice. One wonders what happened to the 14 per cent of NQTs who did not have an assessment report at the end of each term (Totterdell *et al*, 2002). How did the Appropriate Body know how they were doing? Did the NQTs pass their induction period satisfactorily or did the outstanding paperwork mean that they did not? Overall, NQTs are happy with their reports but 7 per cent felt that they were not accurate. One NQT's first term assessment meeting and report did not take place until the end of the second term. Another said: 'I have never seen the written reports.' One headteacher told an NQT at the end of year final assessment meeting that she had failed induction. She had no inkling that this was a possibility and had passed the first two terms' assessments. Again, it shouldn't happen: according to the regulations, the half-termly reviews of progress and termly assessments should give a clear picture. So did the LEA overturn the head's decision? No.

Perhaps you can learn from problems that some people on the *TES* Web site have encountered – and try to avoid having similar things happen to you.

From the *TES forum*

'I had my assessment meeting today. It lasted 10 minutes during my lunch hour! The meeting was just between my induction tutor and me. I was given a copy of the report to read and given a form on which I can write my own comments. I hadn't quite imagined it to be like that.'

This shouldn't happen. Lunchtime is not an ideal time for an assessment meeting. If the NQT is upset by something that has been written, this will have an effect on the afternoon's teaching. The absence of the head (who should have been there), it lasting only 10 minutes, it happening at lunchtime, and the NQT not really having an opportunity to affect what was written at the meeting, all give messages that the assessment and the NQT are not important.

From the **TES forum**
'My school have just realised they have to send a report to the LEA. I haven't had any support from my mentor all term (due to the headteacher delegating everything else to her) and have been struggling to meet my targets on my own. I've only had two weeks with release time this half-term so observations of other staff have gone by the wayside, as have observations of my teaching. There is not time for my review this term so it is being left until 7 January! I just hope I pass.'

I hope situations like this are rare. She could have raised the issue of lack of support and the 10 per cent reduced timetable earlier in the term, with the mentor and head, and then the person in charge of NQTs at the LEA. I would question why there wasn't time for her review. It sounds as if she has low status and the induction regulations have low priority. However, the school is breaking the law in not providing the induction entitlement and she and all the children who are ever going to be taught by her will suffer the consequences. I wouldn't be surprised if this person moved to a school that did value her. Illness should be the only reasons why an assessment meeting and report are postponed. Being busy is a fact of life, highly predictable and so is not an excuse. The school is making itself very vulnerable. The boxes outlining what induction activities have happened should not be ticked and she should word her comment on the assessment form carefully. Perhaps something like this would be appropriate:

I agree with my report. My progress has been hampered by the lack of support that my induction tutor has been able to give me because of her other duties. I have only had a reduced timetable in the weeks of .... I hope that next term I will get release time regularly in order to observe and learn from other colleagues and make progress in developing my teaching.

Top tips!

Q: 'Is there anything I can do to let the LEA know my situation without dropping my school in it?'

A: Professionally worded comments on the assessment form and phone calls to the person in charge of NQTs at the LEA should be made. What you mustn't do is allow your development to suffer – or to risk failing. You are a professional and are expected to speak up for yourself in resolving issues.

Q: 'The induction tutor, whom I never had any sessions with, eventually completed the paperwork for the two terms on my last day at the school. I didn't know that I was able to make any comments on the forms. I was just handed the papers and told to sign them! It was not even original paperwork – they had none in stock and so requested faxed copies from another school and it printed off on the old style shiny fax roll, complete with another school's details across the top...'

A: This is so unprofessional and sloppy! Complain to your head and LEA.

Q: 'Despite the improvements I have made in my classroom management, I have been informed by my induction mentor that I am not making satisfactory progress. I have failed on this area and also because my marking is not up to standard. My HoF told me about the marking two weeks ago and I have been working on it since (prioritising it ahead of planning). My mentor looked at two sets of books, one set was marked well, the other set (a class I struggle to get any work from) was unacceptable. (I've only taught them three times since and they were preparing for and doing a test in that time.) What I need to know is: what should I be writing in the box for my comments? I will be getting advice from my union tomorrow. It is going to be so hard to continue after this. I haven't decided yet what my best course of action is – in the meantime I want to salvage as much as I can from this report.'

A: It really isn't the end of the world to not be deemed to be making satisfactory progress in the first term. I know someone who failed her first term with flying colours and a year later she is stunning and has become a really good induction tutor. In the comment box this

NQT should write that he is making progress on marking and whether he agrees with the report as a whole. People should say what support they think they need (and had/had not in the first term) in order to make clear progress against clear objectives. They should contact the LEA, let them know if there have been any contraventions of the induction entitlement and ask whether there is any extra help. For instance, in Lambeth, primary NQTs can have an Advanced Skills Teacher work with them once a week – it really helps!

Q: 'I'm currently off work with the flu and have not yet had an assessment meeting with my tutor – although I have been told that I have passed the first term. What happens about the forms that need to be filled in and sent off to the LEA? Is there a deadline? Will my first term count?'

A: The weeks before the end of term get very frenetic and people get ill. Since this can be predicted, it's a good idea to be proactive in getting a date for the meeting set before the end of term, so that there is time for it to be rescheduled if necessary. If you or the induction tutor is ill and the meeting doesn't happen or the report doesn't get written, it's not the end of the world. The term will still count towards your induction period. Someone should contact the LEA and let them know that the report will be delayed. You'll need to make sure your assessment report and meeting are at the top of the agenda at the start of the new term, so that your progress is not delayed.

The assessment process should leave you happy to know your strengths and clear about your areas for development. This sets you up well for the rest of your career – your continuing professional development.

The Standards for the Award of Qualified Teacher Status in England

1. Professional Values and Practice

Those awarded Qualified Teacher Status must understand and uphold the professional code of the General Teaching Council for England by demonstrating all of the following:

1.1 They have high expectations of all pupils; respect their social, cultural, linguistic, religious and ethnic backgrounds; and are committed to raising their educational achievement.

1.2 They treat pupils consistently, with respect and consideration, and are concerned for their development as learners.

1.3 They demonstrate and promote the positive values, attitudes and behaviour that they expect from their pupils.

1.4 They can communicate sensitively and effectively with parents and carers, recognising their roles in pupils' learning, and their rights, responsibilities and interests in this.

1.5 They can contribute to, and share responsibly in, the corporate life of schools.

1.6 They understand the contribution that support staff and other professionals make to teaching and learning.

1.7 They are able to improve their own teaching, by evaluating it, learning from the effective practice of others and from evidence. They are motivated and able to take increasing responsibility for their own professional development.

1.8 They are aware of, and work within, the statutory frameworks relating to teachers' responsibilities.

2. Knowledge and Understanding

Those awarded Qualified Teacher Status must demonstrate all of the following:

2.1 They have a secure knowledge and understanding of the subject(s) they are trained to teach. For those qualifying to teach secondary pupils this knowledge and understanding should be at a standard equivalent to degree level. In relation to specific phases, this includes:

a. For the Foundation Stage, they know and understand the aims, principles, six areas of learning and early learning goals described in the QCA/DfEE Curriculum Guidance for the Foundation Stage and, for Reception children, the frameworks, methods and expectations set out in the National Numeracy and Literacy Strategies.

b. For Key Stage 1 and/or 2, they know and understand the curriculum for each of the National Curriculum core subjects, and the frameworks, methods and expectations set out in the National Literacy and Numeracy Strategies. They have sufficient understanding of a range of work across the following subjects:
    - history or geography
    - physical education
    - ICT
    - art and design or design and technology
    - performing arts, and
    - religious education
    to be able to teach them in the age range for which they are trained, with advice from an experienced colleague where necessary.

c. For Key Stage 3, they know and understand the relevant National Curriculum Programme(s) of study, and for those qualifying to teach one or more of the core subjects, the relevant frameworks, methods and expectations set out in the National Strategy for Key Stage 3. All those qualifying to teach a subject at Key Stage 3 know and understand the cross-curricular expectations of the National Curriculum and are familiar with the guidance set out in the National Strategy for Key Stage 3.

d. For Key Stage 4 and post-16, they are aware of the pathways for progression through the 14–19 phase in school, college and work-based settings. They are familiar with the Key Skills as specified by QCA and the national qualifications framework, and they know the progression within and from their own subject and the range of qualifications to which their subject contributes. They understand how courses are combined in students' curricula.

2.2 They know and understand the Values, Aims and Purposes and the General Teaching Requirements set out in the National Curriculum Handbook. As relevant to the age range they are trained to teach, they are familiar with the Programme of Study for Citizenship and the National Curriculum Framework for Personal, Social and Health Education.

2.3 They are aware of expectations, typical curricula and teaching arrangements in the Key Stages or phases before and after the ones they are trained to teach.

2.4 They understand how pupils' learning can be affected by their physical, intellectual, linguistic, social, cultural and emotional development.

2.5 They know how to use ICT effectively, both to teach their subject and to support their wider professional role.

2.6 They understand their responsibilities under the SEN Code of Practice, and know how to seek advice from specialists on less common types of special educational needs.

2.7 They know a range of strategies to promote good behaviour and establish a purposeful learning environment.

2.8 They have passed the Qualified Teacher Status skills tests in numeracy, literacy and ICT.

3.   Teaching

3.1 *Planning, Expectations and Targets*

Those awarded Qualified Teacher Status must demonstrate all of the following:

3.1.1 They set challenging teaching and learning objectives which are relevant to all pupils in their classes. They base these on their knowledge of:
   - the pupils
   - evidence of their past and current achievement
   - the expected standards for pupils of the relevant age range
   - the range and content of work relevant to pupils in that age range.

3.1.2 They use these teaching and learning objectives to plan lessons, and sequences of lessons, showing how they will assess pupils' learning. They take account of and support pupils' varying needs so that girls and boys, from all ethnic groups, can make good progress.

3.1.3 They select and prepare resources, and plan for their safe and effective organisation, taking account of pupils' interests and their language and cultural backgrounds, with the help of support staff where appropriate.

3.1.4 They take part in, and contribute to, teaching teams, as appropriate to the school. Where applicable, they plan for the deployment of additional adults who support pupils' learning.

3.1.5 As relevant to the age range they are trained to teach, they are able to plan opportunities for pupils to learn in out-of-school contexts, such as school visits, museums, theatres, field-work and employment-based settings, with the help of other staff where appropriate.

3.2 Monitoring and Assessment

Those awarded Qualified Teacher Status must demonstrate all of the following:

3.2.1 They make appropriate use of a range of monitoring and assessment strategies to evaluate pupils' progress towards planned learning objectives, and use this information to improve their own planning and teaching.

3.2.2 They monitor and assess as they teach, giving immediate and constructive feedback to support pupils as they learn. They involve pupils in reflecting on, evaluating and improving their own performance.

3.2.3 They are able to assess pupils' progress accurately using, as relevant, the Early Learning Goals, National Curriculum level descriptions, criteria from national qualifications, the requirements of Awarding Bodies, National Curriculum and Foundation Stage assessment frameworks or objectives from the national strategies. They may have guidance from an experienced teacher where appropriate.

3.2.4 They identify and support more able pupils, those who are working below age-related expectations, those who are failing to achieve their potential in learning, and those who experience behavioural, emotional and social difficulties. They may have guidance from an experienced teacher where appropriate.

3.2.5 With the help of an experienced teacher, they can identify the levels of attainment of pupils learning English as an additional language. They begin to analyse the language demands and learning activities in order to provide cognitive challenge as well as language support.

3.2.6 They record pupils' progress and achievements systematically to provide evidence of the range of their work, progress and attainment over time. They use this to help pupils review their own progress and to inform planning.

3.2.7 They are able to use records as a basis for reporting on pupils' attainment and progress orally and in writing, concisely, informatively and accurately for parents, carers, other professionals and pupils.

3.3 *Teaching and Class Management*
Those awarded Qualified Teacher Status must demonstrate all of the following:

3.3.1 They have high expectations of pupils and build successful relationships, centred on teaching and learning. They establish a purposeful learning environment where diversity is valued and where pupils feel secure and confident.

3.3.2 They can teach the required or expected knowledge, understanding and skills relevant to the curriculum for pupils in the age range for which they are trained. In relation to specific phases:

a. those qualifying to teach Foundation Stage children teach all six areas of learning outlined in the QCA/DfEE Curriculum Guidance for the Foundation Stage and, for Reception children, the objectives in the National Literacy and Numeracy Strategy frameworks competently and independently;

b. those qualifying to teach pupils in Key Stage 1 and/or 2 teach the core subjects (English, including the National Literacy Strategy, mathematics through the National Numeracy Strategy, and science) competently and independently. They also teach, for either Key Stage 1 or Key Stage 2, a range of work across the following subjects:
   - history or geography
   - physical education
   - ICT
   - art and design or design and technology, and
   - performing arts

   independently, with advice from an experienced colleague where appropriate;

c. those qualifying to teach Key Stage 3 pupils teach their specialist subject(s) competently and independently using the National Curriculum Programmes of Study for Key Stage 3 and the relevant national frameworks and schemes of work. Those qualifying to teach the core subjects or ICT at Key Stage 3 use the relevant frameworks, methods and expectations set out in the National Strategy for Key Stage 3. All those qualifying to teach a subject at Key Stage 3 must be able to use the cross-curricular elements, such as literacy and numeracy, set out in the National Strategy for Key Stage 3, in their teaching, as appropriate to their specialist subject;

d. those qualifying to teach Key Stage 4 and post–16 pupils teach their specialist subject(s) competently and independently using, as relevant to the subject and age range, the National Curriculum Programmes of Study and related schemes of work, or programmes specified for national qualifications. They also provide opportunities for pupils to develop the key skills specified by QCA.

3.3.3　They teach clearly structured lessons or sequences of work which interest and motivate pupils and which:
- make learning objectives clear to pupils
- employ interactive teaching methods and collaborative group work
- promote active and independent learning that enables pupils to think for themselves, and to plan and manage their own learning.

3.3.4　They differentiate their teaching to meet the needs of pupils, including the more able and those with special educational needs. They may have guidance from an experienced teacher where appropriate.

3.3.5　They are able to support those who are learning English as an additional language, with the help of an experienced teacher where appropriate.

3.3.6　They take account of the varying interests, experiences and achievements of boys and girls, and pupils from different cultural and ethnic groups, to help pupils make good progress.

3.3.7　They organise and manage teaching and learning time effectively.

3.3.8　They organise and manage the physical teaching space, tools, materials, texts and other resources safely and effectively with the help of support staff where appropriate.

3.3.9　They set high expectations for pupils' behaviour and establish a clear framework for classroom discipline to anticipate and manage pupils' behaviour constructively, and promote self-control and independence.

3.3.10　They use ICT effectively in their teaching.

3.3.11　They can take responsibility for teaching a class or classes over a sustained and substantial period of time. They are able to teach across the age and ability range for which they are trained.

3.3.12　They can provide homework and other out-of-class work which consolidates and extends work carried out in the class and encourages pupils to learn independently.

3.3.13　They work collaboratively with specialist teachers and other colleagues and, with the help of an experienced teacher as appropriate, manage the work of teaching assistants or other adults to enhance pupils' learning.

3.3.14　They recognise and respond effectively to equal opportunities issues as they arise in the classroom, including by challenging stereotyped views, and by challenging bullying or harassment, following relevant policies and procedures. (TTA, 2002b)

End of Induction Standard for Wales

In order to complete Induction successfully, the NQT must continue to meet the Standards for the Award of QTS and meet the End of Induction Standard set out here.

1. Professional Characteristics

To meet the End of Induction Standard the NQT must:

1.1 conduct themselves with integrity and apply their knowledge and skills within their professional work;

1.2 reflect on and act to improve their professional practice, taking shared responsibility for their own professional development and learning;

1.3 work collaboratively and cooperatively with those who contribute toward the work of the school;

1.4 demonstrate commitment to equal opportunities, social justice and inclusion.

2. Knowledge and Understanding

To meet the End of Induction Standard the NQT must:

2.1 demonstrate an understanding of practice and the broader educational perspective in Wales when engaging in professional dialogue;

2.2 demonstrate a detailed working knowledge of their sector, the school in which they teach and their related professional responsibilities;

2.3 demonstrate secure knowledge and understanding of the theory and practical skills in the curriculum area or subjects taught;

2.4 deliver the common requirements of the National Curriculum in Wales; that is, communication, mathematical, problem solving, creative and Information Technology skills; Curriculum Cymreig and personal and social development.

3. Planning, Teaching and Learning, and Class Management

To meet the End of Induction Standard the NQT must:

3.1 plan effectively, where applicable, to meet the learning needs of all pupils including those with identified Special Educational Needs, gifted and talented pupils and those with English or Welsh as an Additional Language;

3.2 demonstrate independent thought in selecting and using a broad range of teaching strategies and available resources which they evaluate critically in terms of pupils' learning;

3.3 be able to justify their approach in terms of the curriculum, learning objectives of schemes of work and the learning needs and abilities of their pupils;

4. Monitoring, Assessment and Reporting

To meet the End of Induction Standard the NQT must:

4.1 recognise the level a pupil is achieving and make accurate formative and summative assessments, independently, against attainment targets, where applicable, and performance levels associated with other tests or qualifications relevant to the subject(s) or phases taught;

4.2 record and use the results of day to day assessment to modify their teaching and secure progression in pupils' learning by identifying appropriate learning targets for individuals and groups of pupils;

4.3 provide reports on pupils' progress and achievements, identifying appropriate targets, learning goals and providing guidance to enable parents/carers to support their children's learning.

Scotland's Standard for Full Registration

Professional Knowledge and Understanding

Curriculum

Registered teachers should have detailed knowledge and understanding of the relevant areas of the pre-school, primary or secondary school curriculum.

Registered teachers should have sufficient knowledge and understanding to fulfil their responsibilities for literacy and numeracy; personal, social and health education; and ICT. (As appropriate to the sector and stage of development.)

Registered teachers have a broad, critical understanding of the principal features of the education system, education policy and practice, and of their part in it.

Education Systems and Professional Responsibilities

Registered teachers have a broad, critical understanding of the principal features of the education system, educational policy and practice, and of their part in it.

Registered teachers have detailed working knowledge of their sector, of the school(s) in which they teach, and of their professional responsibilities within them.

Principles and Perspectives

Registered teachers can articulate their professional values and practices and relate them to theoretical principles and perspectives.

Registered teachers have research-based knowledge relating to learning and teaching and a critical appreciation of the contribution of research to education in general.

Professional Skills and Abilities

Teaching and Learning

Registered teachers are able to plan coherent and progressive teaching programmes which match their pupils' needs and abilities, and they can justify what they teach.

Registered teachers communicate clearly, making skilful use of a variety of media, and interact productively with pupils, individually and collectively.

Registered teachers use a range of teaching strategies and resources which they can evaluate and justify in terms of curriculum requirements and of the needs and abilities of their pupils.

Registered teachers set and maintain expectations and pace of work for all pupils.

Registered teachers work co-operatively with other professionals and adults.

Classroom Organisation and Management

Registered teachers organise and manage classes and resources to achieve safe, orderly and purposeful activity.

Registered teachers manage pupil behaviour and classroom incidents fairly, sensitively and consistently, making sensible use of rewards and sanctions, and seeking and using the advice of colleagues when necessary.

Assessment of Pupils

Registered teachers understand and apply the principles of assessment, recording and reporting.

Registered teachers use the results of assessment to evaluate and improve their teaching, and the learning and attainment of the children they teach.

Professional Reflection and Communication

Registered teachers learn from their experience of practice and from critical evaluation of relevant literature in their professional development.

Registered teachers convey an understanding of practice and general educational matters in their professional dialogue and communication.

Registered teachers reflect on and act to improve their own professional practice, contribute to their own professional development, and engage in the process of curriculum development.

Professional Values and Personal Commitment

Registered teachers show in their day-to-day practice a commitment to social justice and inclusion.

Registered teachers take responsibility for their professional learning and development.

Registered teachers value, respect and are active partners in the communities in which they work.

References

Bubb, S. (2000) *The Effective Induction of Newly Qualified Primary Teachers: An Induction Tutor's Handbook*, David Fulton, London.

Bubb, S. (2001) *A Newly Qualified Teacher's Manual: How to Meet the Induction Standards*, David Fulton, London.

Bubb, S. and Mulholland, M. (2003) *Overseas Trained Teacher Portfolio*, Institute of Education, London.

Bubb, S., Heilbronn, R., Jones, C., Totterdell, M. and Bailey, M. (2002) *Improving Induction: Research-based Best Practice*, Routledge Falmer, London.

Clarke, S. (2001) *Unlocking Formative Assessment*, Hodder & Stoughton, London.

Department for Education and Employment (1999) Circular 4/99: 'Physical and mental fitness to teach of teachers and of entrants to initial teacher training', DfEE, London.

Department for Education and Skills (2000) *The Induction Period for Newly Qualified Teachers*, DfES, London.

Department for Education and Skills (2001) *The Standards' Framework*, DfES, London.

Department for Education and Skills (2002a) *School Teachers' Pay and Conditions*, DfES, London.

Department for Education and Skills (2003a) *Guidance on Induction*, DfES, London.

Earley, P. and Kinder, K. (1994) *Initiation Rights: Effective Induction Practices for New Teachers*, NFER, Slough.

Emmerson, I. (2000) 'One mistake and you're out', *Times Educational Supplement*, 17 November, pp. 30–31.

Flynn, F. (2001) *Get Your First Job*, TES, London.

Furlong, J. and Maynard, T. (1995) *Mentoring Student Teachers: A Practical Guide*, Falmer Press, London.

Hastings, N. and Chantrey-Wood, K. (2002) *Reorganising Primary Classroom Learning*, Open University Press, Milton Keynes.

OFSTED (2000) *Inspecting Schools*, OFSTED, London.

Stern, J. (1999) *Learning to Teach*, David Fulton, London.

Student Loans Company (2002) *Repayment of Student Loans for Teachers of Shortage Subjects*, SLC, London.

Teacher Training Agency (2001) *The Role of Induction Tutor: Principles and Guidance*, TTA, London.

Teacher Training Agency (2002a) *Supporting Induction for Newly Qualified Teachers*, TTA, London.

Teacher Training Agency (2002b) *Qualifying to Teach: Professional Standards for Qualified Teacher Status and Requirements for Initial Teacher Training*, TTA, London.

Teacher Training Agency (2002c) *Qualifying to Teach: Handbook of Guidance*, TTA, London.

Teacher Training Agency (2002d) *Numeracy and Literacy QTS Skills Test: Report on the National Results for the Academic Year 2000–01*, TTA, London.

Teacher Training Agency (2002e) *ITT Performance Profiles 2001*, TTA, London.

Teacher Training Agency (2003a) *How to Qualify as a Teacher in England: A Guide for Overseas Trained Teachers*, TTA, London.

Teacher Training Agency (2003b) *The Career Entry and Development Profile*, TTA, London.

Totterdell, M., Heilbronn, R., Bubb, S. and Jones, C. (2002) 'Evaluation of the effectiveness of the statutory arrangements for the induction of newly qualified teachers', research brief and report No. 338, DfES, London.

Index